ONE DAY
AT A TIME

Discovering the Freedom
of 12-Step Spirituality

TREVOR HUDSON

UPPER
ROOM BOOKS®
NASHVILLE

ONE DAY AT A TIME
Discovering the Freedom of 12-Step Spirituality
© 2007 by Trevor Hudson. All rights reserved.

Upper Room®, Upper Room Books®, and design logos are trademarks owned by The Upper Room®, a Ministry of GBOD®, Nashville, Tennessee. All rights reserved.

The Upper Room Web site: http://www.upperroom.org

This book was originally published as *One Day at a Time* © 2005, by Trevor Hudson by Struik Christian Books, A division of New Holland Publishing (South Africa) (Pty) Ltd., 80 McKenzie Street, Cape Town 8001, South Africa.

Page 142 constitutes an extension of this copyright page.

Cover design: Bruce Gore/GoreStudio
Cover illustration: Nicholas Wilton/Stock Illustration Source
First printing: 2007

LIBRARY OF CONGRESS CATALOGING-IN-PUBLICATION DATA
Hudson, Trevor, 1951–
   One day at a time: discovering the freedom of 12-step spirituality / Trevor Hudson.
   p. cm.
   Originally published: Cape Town. South Africa: Struik Christian Books, 2005.
   ISBN 978-0-8358-9913-0
   1. Twelve-step programs—Religious aspects—Christianity. 2. Spirituality. I. Title
   BV4596.T88H83 2007
   248.8'629—dc22   2007030100
Printed in the United States of America

To Debbie, Joni, and Mark—
special gifts from God
and
to Bill Meaker—patient encourager
in all my writing efforts

CONTENTS

ACKNOWLEDGMENTS

Thank you to the team at Upper Room Books, especially Stephen Bryant, Kathleen Stephens, Rita Collett, and Robin Pippin, for their encouragement and colleagueship in the ministry of books. Their efforts in getting this book out for North American readers is deeply appreciated.

Thank you to Bill Meaker for his careful reading of each chapter and helpful suggestions. Over the years he has continually challenged me to write in a more simple, down-to-earth and practical way.

Thank you to John H. from Alcoholics Anonymous who companioned me throughout the writing of this book. Constantly he would bring to my attention some aspect of AA thinking that I had overlooked. His personal recovery and way of life bears powerful witness to the way God uses the Twelve Step program to restore and to heal.

Thank you to Keith Miller, who through his many writings, has shaped my thinking considerably when it comes to linking the Twelve Steps with the Christian faith. To this day I continue to read and reread his material as I seek to work the Steps in my own life. I would love to say thank you in person one day.

Thank you to Lyn Meyer for her faithful colleagueship in preparing this manuscript for the publisher. I am in debt to her for her generous willingness to invest talents and time in each book that I write.

Thank you to all my friends at AA who often share their experience, strength, hope, and counsel with me.

Thank you to my church family at Northfield Methodist Church, especially to my colleagues Schalk Pienaar, John and Debbie van de Laar, and Phidian Matsepe for their interaction and conversation around some of the ideas presented in this book.

Lastly, but not least, thank you to Debbie, Joni, and Mark, with whom I share my life as a "recovering sinner." Their faithful love helps me more than anything else in the world to experience the faithful love of God.

FINDING THE POWER
TO LIVE FOR A CHANGE

This book has been written for those who want to change. It is for men and women who feel the need to deepen their lives, to live more freely, to be happier. If you are not sure whether this includes you, let me be a little more specific: *One Day at a Time* has been written especially for those

- *who worry too much*—whose waking hours are plagued by all kinds of fears (about the future, about their relationships, about their children, about their health, about their finances) and who sometimes waken in the middle of the night with an anxious knot in their stomach and cannot get back to sleep.
- *who struggle with some form of compulsive and addictive behavior*—perhaps an addiction to a substance like alcohol, drugs, or tranquilizers; or perhaps to activities like making money, gambling, working too hard, watching TV soaps, online chats, computer games, shopping, sex, or even going to church every night of the week.
- *who battle with increasing levels of stress and tension*—those who feel that they cannot cope with the demands being made upon them, who feel that their energy resources have been depleted and that they cannot handle any more pressure.

- *who sabotage their relationships with destructive patterns of behavior*—things like trying to control others too much, withdrawing into sulky silences, blowing up in anger, always trying to "fix" those around them, or getting stuck in the mud of their resentments.

- *who feel trapped by feelings of self-condemnation, guilt, and regret*—who are weighed down by secret sins and baggage from the past; who constantly hear in their heads those inner, shaming voices, saying, "You are no good! You are not acceptable! You will never amount to anything! You are beyond redemption!"

- *who may worship on a regular basis but somehow feel that their faith has become bogged down in pious clichés and empty ritual*—those who long for a living and vital spirituality that leads toward the transformation of their personal lives and the environments in which they live, work, and play.

If you can identify with any of these descriptions, take heart. There is hope. There are others like you, and many of them are discovering a new depth and freedom and joy in their daily lives. How they are finding this power to live for a change is what this book is all about.

THE POWER DILEMMA

When we look around today, we see that in spite of all the self-help books and self-fulfillment techniques flooding the market human misery abounds. There remain in our midst in ever-increasing numbers sad incidents of despair, suicide, addiction, violence, corruption, and personal emptiness, and what seems to be a tragic inability to get along even with those we say we love. Massive social changes, even those for the better, seem unable to transform the hearts of men and women. Clearly, when it comes to inner change, human resources alone are not sufficient. We need a power from beyond ourselves.

There is good news! Those who wrote God's Good Book were unanimous about one thing: *There is available to all of us as human beings a Power greater than ourselves*—a power that can inwardly change us, that can set us free from life-spoiling habits and addictions, that can help us grow into better people; that can help us heal relationships, that can equip us to make a creative difference where we live and work. It is a power that enables us to know the living presence of God in our lives. However, if we want to experience this life-changing power, we need to learn how to plug into it.

In the following pages I will show you one way to do this. While this way may surprise you, it is not original. It draws from one of the most powerful programs for change and spiritual progress ever devised: the *Twelve Step program* made famous by Alcoholics Anonymous. The Twelve Step process is an experience of being changed by a caring and powerful God who knows what we need—a God who is able to reach deep inside our lives and change us for the better. I hope that, as you explore and follow these steps, they will become as helpful to you as they have been to me.

MAPPING
OUR JOURNEY

You may be wondering how I, a nonalcoholic, came across the Twelve Step program. Allow me to share a little bit of my story with you.

Over the years I have struggled with the need for change in many areas of my life. When I was younger, I battled with an addiction to gambling in the area of horse racing. Twenty-five years of marriage have brought home the subtle depths of my own self-centeredness. Moments of extreme tiredness have exposed compulsive tendencies to overwork and overcommit. My children, especially, have helped me to recognize how hard I find it to lighten up and really enjoy myself. These issues and others as well have caused much heartache and pain and struggle—not only for myself but also for those around me.

However, while wrestling with this need for change I discovered the helpfulness of the Twelve Step program. Here is how it happened.

Some of my friends happen to be recovering alcoholics. We often get together to talk about the struggles and joys of our lives. Whenever I spoke about my own compulsions and character defects, like those mentioned above, they would point me toward the program. One day a friend told me bluntly, "Trevor,

just work the Twelve Steps." I began to do so and have continued it on a day-by-day basis, even now. This is how I came to
discover the power and value of the Twelve Step program.

When I look back over this time, I can see clearly that the
Twelve Steps have become God's surprising way of keeping my
life on track. I have little doubt that without the wisdom and
practical guidance they offer my life would have been very much
poorer today at every level. They have given me a way of dealing with my tendency toward compulsive behavior, helped me
take a closer look at my weaknesses and provided me with practical tools for spiritual growth and healing. In a nutshell, the
Twelve Steps have become profoundly helpful in my own ongoing personal journey of change.

However, I should not really have been surprised. Literally
millions of people around the world can testify to the blessings
and benefits of working the Twelve Step program, not just in
Alcoholics Anonymous but in many other recovery and healing
programs. These wonderful gifts include things like peace of
mind, newfound freedom, and the joy found in serving others.
Furthermore, they have provided for many people a solid and
realistic plan for growing spiritually. Small wonder that Dallas
Willard, one of the most respected spiritual writers of our time,
comments in one of his books: *"Any successful plan for spiritual
formation, whether for the individual or group, will in fact be
significantly similar to the Alcoholics Anonymous program."*[1]

THE TWELVE STEPS

You may not be familiar with the Twelve Steps. The person
largely responsible for formulating them was Bill W., one of the
founding members of Alcoholics Anonymous. During the spring

of 1938, when he was writing the story of the AA movement, he listed twelve principles that he believed helped alcoholics to recover. They had grown out of his own experience and that of other alcoholics from what he had learned from an evangelical movement called the Oxford Group and from his reading of the Bible, especially the Sermon on the Mount. They eventually became known as the Twelve Step program. While I will be adapting those steps that speak specifically of alcoholism, here are the Twelve Steps as they are used in AA:

1. We admitted we were powerless over alcohol—that our lives had become unmanageable.
2. Came to believe that a Power greater than ourselves could restore us to sanity.
3. Made a decision to turn our will and our lives over to the care of God *as we understood God.*
4. Made a searching and fearless moral inventory of ourselves.
5. Admitted to God, to ourselves, and to another human being the exact nature of our wrongs.
6. Were entirely ready to have God remove all these defects of character.
7. Humbly asked God to remove our shortcomings.
8. Made a list of all persons we had harmed, and became willing to make amends to them all.
9. Made direct amends to such people wherever possible, except when to do so would injure them or others.
10. Continued to take personal inventory and, when we were wrong, promptly admitted it.
11. Sought through prayer and meditation to improve our conscious contact with God *as we understood God,* praying

only for knowledge of God's will for us and the power to carry that out.

12. Having had a spiritual awakening as a result of these steps, we tried to carry this message to alcoholics and to practice these principles in all our affairs.

If you study each of these steps carefully, you will see that the program is deeply, though not specifically, Christian. Steps One, Two, and Three invite us to give up our natural tendency to want to be in total control—to be managing directors—and instead to let God be God in our lives. Steps Four, Five, and Ten call on us constantly to examine our lives and to confess our wrongs. Steps Six and Seven prompt us to let God change us from the inside out. The Eighth and Ninth Steps encourage us to mend broken relationships wherever we can. The Eleventh Step shows us how to grow in our relationship with God on a daily basis. Last, but not least, the Twelfth Step challenges us to share the hope of recovery with other strugglers and sufferers. Can you see how close these steps are to the spirit of Jesus of Nazareth and the writings of the New Testament?

What is most important is that the Twelve Step program be seen as a way of life, not just a set of rules. It does not offer us a theory for change, but a way of living, rooted deeply in the biblical wisdom that leads to change. These steps are not meant to be done once, and then checked off as completed, never to be done again. They are steps to be taken regularly, sometimes several times in one day. We must not just think about them; we must do them. As AA's Big Book reminds us: "The spiritual life is not a theory. *We have to live it.*"[2]

In reflecting on these Twelve Steps from the perspective of someone who is not an alcoholic, I hope that I have been faithful to the spirit and content of the Alcoholics Anonymous program. If you are already involved in AA or some other recovery group, please don't change what you are doing. However, if you sense that God may be nudging you toward living for a change and you are not too sure how to go about it, I hope these steps will guide and help you. May they also draw you into a more personal and living relationship with God and enable you to live with greater joy and freedom and serenity.

In closing, this book should be seen as a companion to *The Serenity Prayer*,[3] which is a series of meditations that I wrote on that prayer. Together, these two books express my gratitude to Alcoholics Anonymous for the way it has helped throw light on biblical treasures sometimes neglected by the Christian church. I also hope that these two books together will make available to a wider audience the spiritual wisdom contained in these wonderful treasures.

STEP ONE

We admitted we were powerless over alcohol—that our lives had become unmanageable.

I do not understand my own actions. For I do not do what I want, but I do the very thing I hate. . . . I can will what is right, but I cannot do it.
—Romans 7:15, 18

THE COURAGE
TO CHANGE

There is one subject that we tend to avoid. Strangely, it is not the subject of sex or money or politics or death or even religion. What we often prefer not to talk about openly is the topic of our weaknesses. We are seldom prepared to discuss this aspect of our lives honestly—not even with our loved ones or close friends. We would much rather dodge the issue. When someone asks how we are doing, our usual answer is, "Fine, thank you."

There are a number of reasons why this is so. To begin with, the word *weakness* has negative connotations. We tend to think negatively about people we consider to be weak-willed or weak-kneed or weak-minded. They are the losers, the ones who are usually defeated, the unfortunates who lack what it takes to succeed. In today's society such people are looked down upon. We do not want to be thought of in this way.

Another reason might be that, from an early age, many of us are taught to be strong, especially those of us who are male. We receive a clear message: The successful are those who are in control, who have it all together. Even if we are not on top of things, it becomes important to pretend that we are. And so we continually try to look stronger or smarter or more successful than we really are. We cannot mention our weaknesses too loudly. The weak perish, we are told, and only the strong survive.

A third reason could simply be that we are often quite blind to our own weaknesses. Usually we prefer to notice them in others. Or we deny them. Or we try to rationalize them away. We have a remarkable capacity for self-delusion and denial. When confronted about our failures, we say something like, "I don't know what came over me. I just wasn't myself." Quite frankly, what comes over us are our weaknesses, whatever they may be.

The wonderful news is that we can live beyond our weaknesses. They are the place where new life can often break forth. In other words, we do not have to remain stuck. There is a tried and tested program for us to grow and to change into better people. The Twelve Step program, as some have called it, is available to everyone. It's down to earth, practical, and filled with biblical wisdom. But before we can begin to experience its benefits and blessings, there is an important precondition. We first need to admit our weaknesses. So let me ask you, are you someone who is willing to do this?

I have put together a simple, homemade "Quick Quiz" to help you think about this question. You might go through it quickly, answering each question with a simple yes or no.

QUICK QUIZ

- Do you struggle to admit to problems when you have them?
- Do you struggle to ask others for help?
- Do you find it easier to serve than to be served?
- Are you afraid to cry, to show deep emotion?

- Would you struggle against going for counseling?
- Do you tend to blame others for your failures?
- Do you sometimes wear a mask of self-sufficiency and confidence?
- Do you struggle to listen without judgment when others speak of their weaknesses and failures?
- Are you sometimes too tired to keep running and too scared to stop?
- Are you reluctant to go to the doctor when you are not feeling well?

How did it go? If you answered yes to some of these questions, it could be that you are one of the many who find it difficult to admit their weaknesses. If so, would you allow the wisdom of the first step of the Twelve Step program to speak to you? It is a wisdom that comes directly from the pages of the Bible and can be summarized like this:

The first step toward change involves a courageous admission of our weaknesses.

When we cannot take this first step, we cut ourselves off from the experience of God's power changing us from the inside out.

Let us, then, try to explore the subject of our weaknesses more deeply.

EXPLORING OUR WEAKNESSES

What do we mean when we speak of weaknesses? I have in mind those things that repeatedly defeat us, that spoil our lives and our relationships, that we cannot seem to fix in our own strength. Those things over which, in the words of the Twelve Step program, we seem to be powerless and that make our lives unmanageable. I will give some specific examples. Perhaps you will be able to identify these weaknesses in your own life.

First and foremost, there is the weakness of our *will*. There is little doubt in my mind that the human will is God's most precious gift to us. It represents that deepest part of who we are, that inner place where all our choices and decisions are made. Yet, often our human will is also extremely limited. Just think of the many times you have resolved to do the right and good thing but have failed. Even one of the greatest spiritual giants struggled in this regard. "What I don't understand about myself," Paul wrote, "is that I decide one way, but then I act another, doing things I absolutely despise" (Rom. 7:15, THE MESSAGE). Does this dilemma ring a bell with your experience?

Second, there is the weakness of our *addictive behavior*. It is not only the alcoholic or drug abuser who is an addict. In one way or another, many of us struggle with some form of addictive behavior. Think of the various substances on which we can so easily become dependent. These range from the more pleasurable ones like caffeine, chocolate, and sweets, to the more dangerous like diet pills and tranquilizers. Other activities can take over our lives, like gambling, making money, work, helping others, physical exercise, watching pornography, or overeating, to name a few. Some people have become hooked on the Internet and on playing computer games.

You may resist the notion that you are an addict. If you do, there is a simple test to check whether you are hooked on a substance or activity. If you say to yourself, "I can handle it" or "I can do without it," then go ahead and stop taking the substance or taking part in the activity. If you cannot, excuses or rationalizations will not change the fact that you are addicted.

Third, there is the weakness of *habitual wrongdoing*. Deep down we all know the difference between right and wrong, good and bad. Most of us will agree that it is better to give than to steal, to build than to destroy, to be faithful than to cheat. Yet we all know how easy it is for us to get caught up in actions that we know are wrong. These ways of behaving can sometimes bring us into bondage. Although we try to break away from them, we fail repeatedly, and often end up in a place of deep guilt and shame and despair.

Fourth, there is the weakness of *negative feelings*. By this I mean those destructive emotions that we would like to change but cannot. It could be a continual sense of worry, an overwhelming anxiety, a deep fearfulness. Or it might be powerful feelings of anger and aggression that cause us to explode, sometimes over something small and trivial. Perhaps one of the most damaging of all our feelings is resentment. Few things injure our emotional and physical health more than this one. No wonder in AA's Big Book, resentment emerges as one of the main sources of futility and unhappiness.

PAINFUL CONSEQUENCES

A reluctance to admit our weaknesses has several painful consequences. On the one hand, we often find ourselves living a lie. We hide behind masks of competence and self-sufficiency and pretend we are OK. We become actors in the drama of our lives, playing roles far removed from who we really are. People around us, especially those nearest and dearest to us, feel we have put up a barrier and that they cannot reach us or get close to us. This can isolate us from real contact and openness with others. Always pretending to have it together makes for lonely living, which can be very painful indeed.

On the other hand, when they are not admitted, our weaknesses can become much more destructive. When, for example, we do not acknowledge the weakness of the human will, we could become even more entangled in conflicting desires and wants. Hidden addiction increases its vicelike grip. Concealed habitual wrongdoing causes increasing havoc in our lives and relationships. Suppressed negative feelings get stronger and more oppressive. Small wonder that those in the recovery movement remind us that we are as sick as our secrets. Unacknowledged weaknesses have a scary way of gradually taking over our lives, robbing us of joy and freedom and peace of mind.

However, there can be a positive side to these painful consequences. They can make us aware that we are often powerless to change ourselves and that we do not have all the power and self-control that we once thought we did. We are not always able, in our own strength and willpower, to fix everything that is broken in our lives. We are finite human beings with definite limitations who need a power from beyond ourselves to help us live freely and fully. In the end, it is often the pain caused by our divided human will, our addictions, our habitual wrongdoing, and our negative feelings that helps us make this important discovery and finally let go of our do-it-yourself recovery attempts.

You might be on the verge of discovering this for yourself. As you look back on a string of repeated attempts to change an area of personal weakness, all your efforts may seem to have been in vain. They have not brought the freedom and happiness that you have been looking for. You can see clearly that, when it comes to this particular struggle, you are not really in control. You are at a place where you are willing to acknowledge that your life has become unmanageable. If this describes where you are right now, perhaps you are ready to take the first step.

INTO ACTION

Admitting the reality of our weaknesses is the first and most important step on the journey toward change. Without it there can be little progress. This admission includes, as we have seen, facing up to our limited ability to change ourselves. Taking this step seldom comes easily. It requires great courage, humility, and honesty. And we will most likely have to take it more than once. We may never reach a point where we can say, "All my weaknesses are now behind me. I have finally arrived." There are always weaknesses to be admitted. If we continue to be honest and real, we will never stop growing and changing.

If you feel you are ready to take this first step, try to be as specific as you can. Naming our weakness is a powerful act. It brings hidden struggles out into the open. It opens up a little daylight between them and ourselves. It connects us with those who battle in a similar way. Most importantly, putting our personal weakness into words by naming it indicates our willingness to accept that, if we are going to change in this area, we must look to a power greater than ourselves for help.

One way of taking this first step is to copy out the following statement on a piece of paper and then to complete it by filling in our name and area of personal weakness on the underlines.

> I, _____, *admit that I am powerless*
> *over*_____ *and that my life has*
> *become unmanageable.*

Sharing this statement with a trusted friend often brings a sense of greater realism to our desire for change.

When we admit our weaknesses in this way, we discover one of the greatest secrets of the spiritual journey—that in our weakness lies our strength. This is one of the most powerful spiritual truths that we will ever discover. Rather than rejecting us because of our weaknesses, it opens the door for God to come alongside us and help us overcome what had previously defeated us. God's strength can lead us beyond our weakness and enable us to grow spiritually strong. It is where we limp the most that we can experience the power of God. This is why, many hundreds of years ago, one well-known recovering sinner once wrote, "If I must boast, I will boast of the things that show my weakness. . . . For when I am weak, then I am strong" (2 Cor. 11:30; 12:10, NIV).

Are you willing to set out on this exciting adventure toward becoming a person who is freer, happier, and more alive? It begins when you have the courage to accept your need for change, name the weakness that constantly gets the better of you, and acknowledge that you cannot fix it in your own strength. When you take this step as fully as possible, you are ready to embark on the journey of change and spiritual growth.

TAKING IT FURTHER IN GROUP SHARING

1. Share your results from the "Quick Quiz."
2. With which of the four categories of weakness can you identify?
3. When have you experienced God's power in an area of personal weakness? How did this happen?
4. What is your response to the invitation to take Step One?

STEP TWO

We came to believe that a Power greater than ourselves could restore us to sanity.

Jesus said to him, "If you are able!—All things can be done for the one who believes." Immediately the father of the child cried out, "I believe; help my unbelief!"

—Mark 9:23-24

HOPE FOR CHANGE

Some time ago I sat with a middle-aged man who had come to speak to me about a problem that was slowly destroying his life. A secret sexual addiction had already cost him his marriage, estranged him from his children, and filled him with a deep sense of shameful guilt. Repeated failures to overcome this struggle had left him in the darkness of extreme despair. As he finished telling me his story, he looked straight at me and asked, "Do you really believe that anything or anyone can help me to change?"

This question often comes to the surface when we begin to face up to those weaknesses that are getting the better of us. Whether it is when we acknowledge the weakness of our will-power, our addictions, our bad habits, or our negative feelings, facing up to those things that repeatedly defeat us can sometimes make us feel hopeless. It can even bring us to the very edge of depression. We seriously begin to wonder whether we will ever find the power to be different or whether we are doomed to remain trapped in the dark prison of our weaknesses for ever. Perhaps you will know from your own experience what I am trying to describe.

The Second Step of the Twelve Step program shines a bright ray of light into this darkness. It boldly tells us that there is a solution—a solution that can empower us to deal creatively with our weaknesses, a solution that can help us to live with a new freedom and joy and sanity, a solution that comes from beyond ourselves and has a deep spiritual dimension. This is the incredible offer of the Second Step. Not surprisingly, some have called it "the Hope Step." Here is my summarized version of the promised solution:

> *There is a Higher Power available to each one of us that can help us to live more freely and fully.*

Let us explore a little further what this is saying.

A POWER GREATER THAN OURSELVES

If you eavesdrop at your local AA meeting, you will sometimes hear those present talking about their "Higher Power." Most people there would probably understand this phrase to mean God and would be prepared to allow some flexibility in how others may understand God. For a few recovering alcoholics, however, this phrase might not even mean God. It could refer to the power of the group itself, or to the power of nature, or to the power of the universe, and so on.

I know Christians who are uncomfortable with allowing for these various meanings. They feel that it can lead people away from what is true and that we speak more directly about God. As a result, they may turn away from using the Twelve Step program. This is a great pity because they rob themselves of valuable insights about how they can change and grow into the people that God wants them to be. After all, many of those who find help through the Twelve Steps are people whom the church has not been able to reach. I can understand why those who formulated the Twelve Step program did not try to define the Higher Power. They were aware that people could be at different stages of the journey to discovering who God is and did not want this to be a barrier. Some alcoholics might even have been deeply hurt by the way the church and other religious organizations had judged them. Others might be agnostics or atheists. If the Second Step had demanded a particular standard of belief, it might easily have become an obstruction to their attempt to stop drinking. Allowing them the freedom to find their own understanding of their Higher Power meant that they could still be part of the program while moving on at their own pace. Wonderfully, because of their positive experiences with the Twelve Steps, most alcoholics do come to a deeper understanding of and belief in a loving and caring God who can help us change.

There are two other reasons the term *Higher Power* can be helpful, especially when we use it to refer to God. On the one hand, the phrase reminds us that God is always much greater than the weaknesses that continually defeat us. This perspective breathes hope into the dark despair we often feel when we are not coping. For when we come to believe that God is bigger than the things we are battling with, we are given courage to believe that we will be able to change and endure whatever it is we are facing. Acknowledging this possibility can be an enormous source of hope in times of struggle.

Second, this phrase reminds us that God is an unseen spiritual presence and power. Hence, when we speak about getting help from God, we are talking about receiving resources from beyond ourselves. The phrase opens us to the possibilities of prayer and to the wisdom and strength that come from a "higher" source than merely our own human cleverness and power. Maybe this is one reason why an ancient prophet once quoted God as saying, "As the heavens are *higher* than the earth, so are my ways *higher* than your ways and my thoughts than your thoughts" (Isa. 55:9, RSV; emphasis mine).

In this day and age, when we tend to refer to God in very familiar and superficial ways, these two reasons underline the advantages of the descriptive phrase *Higher Power*. It can be a helpful corrective to our tragic tendency to fashion God into some kind of manageable deity that we can control whenever we want to: a small god, as it were, that we can put into our back pockets when we no longer need him. In vivid contrast, when we refer to God as our Higher Power we realize that we *are* dealing with a spiritual reality who is always greater than what we happen to be struggling with—Someone full of mystery in whose presence we always need to stand in awe and wonder.

RESTORES US TO SANITY

One more thing needs to be said about this Higher Power. We need to have some idea of what kind of power it is. Is this Higher Power *for* us or *against* us? This is an important issue because many people carry negative pictures of God with them. They see God as someone who is always out to get them. They believe that God is vengeful, vindictive, and punishing. Perhaps you do too. Now if this is your picture of God, you will probably want to keep God at a distance. Fortunately, the second half of Step Two gives us an important clue about the nature of this Higher Power. It is a wonderful bit of good news. God wants only the best for us. God is genuinely interested in restoring us to being the way we were meant to be. Go back for a moment to the Second Step. It reads: "We came to believe that a Power greater than ourselves *could restore us to sanity*" (emphasis mine). Take a few moments to think about these last words. They point to a Higher Power who is on our side—who cares about us; who wants to help us change for the better; who is always reaching out to us, wanting to make something beautiful out of the brokenness of our lives. This is how recovering alcoholics have experienced this Higher Power, and it is what we also need to discover for ourselves.

"But I am not insane," I can hear you saying, "and I do not need my sanity restored!" I can understand why you might respond like this. Usually the word *insanity* conjures up images of Jack Nicholson playing the part of a mental patient in *One Flew over the Cuckoo's Nest*! We may have problems, we think to ourselves, but we are certainly not insane. If this is what you are thinking, keep reading for a little longer as I try to describe what sanity and insanity may look like in our lives.

Sanity describes a state in which we think and behave in a balanced, healthy, and life-giving way. *Insanity* is when we think and behave in ways that are not balanced and healthy and when we constantly make choices that undermine our well-being. In extreme cases, this behavior may indicate deep mental disorder that needs special treatment or being cared for in an institution. But there are other, subtler ways in which we lose the ability to think clearly and behave rationally. At times we do not respond in balanced and healthy ways, and other forces seem to be in control of our lives. Insanity, my friends from AA keep telling me, is continually repeating destructive patterns of thought and behavior in spite of the problems they may be causing us.

This definition takes insanity out of the world of padded cells and white-coated doctors and puts it right back in the middle of ordinary, everyday life. It brings to mind all those self-defeating things that we keep on thinking or doing, even though they are spoiling our lives and our relationships; those crazy things that we know, even while we are doing them, are not balanced and healthy. Think, for example, of how we sometimes keep on

- blaming everyone and everything for our problems;
- trying to control those around us, and getting them to do what we want;
- giving loved ones the silent treatment when we are angry with them;
- putting off important things that need to be done;
- harboring hate and thoughts of revenge over things that have been said or done to us;
- blowing up angrily over things that have not gone our way;
- talking incessantly and seldom listening to what others are saying;
- gambling obsessively to the detriment of caring for our families;
- taking on more and more commitments at work, even when we are overcommitted;
- buying things that we do not really need and that place our lives under increased financial pressure.

The list of possibly "insane" thoughts and behavior goes on and on. Perhaps these few examples can help you assess your own patterns of self-destructive behavior and thinking. Most of us cannot see our insanity right away. Either we are blind at times, or we do not want to acknowledge these things for fear that we will have to take responsibility for our actions. However, when we do catch a glimpse of our self-defeating ways of thinking and acting, it can make us either laugh or cry. Yet the one thing we do not have to give in to is despair. There is a Higher Power who wants to help us restore our lives to sanity. The big question is, Are we willing to believe this?

INTO ACTION

I really like the way the Second Step is set out. It says, "We *came* to believe . . ." Those who wrote these words obviously knew that the journey to a real faith is a process that often takes time and that people are at different places on this journey. It does not all happen overnight. While there are most certainly some people who have dramatic spiritual experiences, most of us come to believe in much quieter and less spectacular ways. Sometimes we cannot even say exactly when it was that we came to believe in a power greater than ourselves, but we know deep down that we do.

In our search for a living faith, we can learn a great deal from scientists. They realize that they do not know everything about the physical, material world, and so they experiment. They try one thing and then another until they find the answer they seek. In the initial stages, the process of finding a real faith can follow a very similar method. We can make an assumption that God is real, try it out in our own way, and then weigh up the results. When we do this with an open and honest attitude, we will begin to discover in our own experience the reality of God's unseen spiritual presence and power.

Can you see now what it means to take the Second Step? It opens our minds to the possibility that there is a God who wants to help us to live a changed life. We can begin to tell God honestly about the weaknesses that are getting the better of us. We can ask for the strength to think and act in healthier and more balanced ways. We can start getting together with other spiritual seekers who also want to grow in faith. As we embark on our own experiments of faith, what we will discover is that what we receive over a period of time may not necessarily be flashes of blinding light and a quick fix but rather a sense of growing inner strength, greater sanity and peace of mind—a quiet realization that there is hope for our situation, no matter what we are facing.

Perhaps you are ready to take this step now. If you are, may I suggest you write out a simple statement that expresses your willingness to begin taking seriously the availability of a power greater than yourself to restore your life to sanity. You might like to use the following sentence, filling in the blanks with your name and the particular problem that is getting the better of you at the moment.

> I, _____, am willing from this day onward to begin living on the basis that God wants to help me to change, especially when it comes to my struggle with _____ (name any particular weakness).

There really is hope for change. Our problems need not have the final say about the outcome of our lives. There is *Someone* who wants to help us to live a freer and fuller life. The Big Book of AA suggests that as soon as we say we believe this or are willing to believe this, we will have started on our journey toward those changes that will lead us to spiritual growth and personal happiness.[1] In a nutshell, we will begin to experience a growing sense of sanity and strength that we have not known before, and we will know deep down that we have taken another step along the way toward real and lasting inner transformation.

TAKING IT FURTHER IN GROUP SHARING

1. Do you find it helpful or unhelpful to think of God as a "Higher Power"?
2. Share your response to the list of insane things that we keep doing and thinking.
3. Describe your present level of belief in God.
4. What is your response to the invitation to take Step Two?

STEP THREE

*We made a decision to turn our will
and our lives over to the care
of God as we understood God.*

Trust in the LORD with all your heart,
    and do not rely on your own insight.
In all your ways acknowledge him,
    and he will make straight your paths.
        —Proverbs 3:5-6, RSV

DECISION TIME

I want to turn the spotlight on one of the most important decisions that you and I can ever make. It is a decision that brings us alive in our relationship with God—a decision that opens our hands to receive God's gifts of peace and forgiveness, a decision that releases God's power into those areas where we have constantly struggled and failed. Perhaps most significantly, it is a decision that gives our lives a new center and focus from which a brand-new person can begin to emerge. The decision goes like this. Are you ready?

> *To give up "playing God" and to surrender ourselves*
> *as completely as we can to God.*

This decision, which lies at the heart of the Third Step, does not come easily. It goes against the grain of some of our most powerful natural instincts. Since childhood our lives seem to be dominated by the assumption that "I am the center of the universe and everything and everyone should revolve around my wishes, my desires, my interests, and my needs." We want to be in control or feel that we ought to be in control of everything that has to do with our lives. Rather than letting God be God, we try to play the part of God ourselves. It is no wonder that we resist so strongly the idea of handing over our lives to God.

The Big Book of AA supplies a helpful image.[1] It suggests that you and I are like actors who want to run the whole show our own way. We want to arrange the lights, the play, the scenery, and the rest of the actors. We want to tell them what to do, how they should say their lines and play their parts. We believe that if everyone would only do as we want them to, the show would be great. What usually happens, however, is that the show does not go off too well. Other people do not do what we want them to do. And so we become more demanding and controlling and are angry that the other actors do not play their parts as we think they should.

The story in Genesis 3:1–7 depicts how self-centeredness and the need to be in control at all times are the cause of so much trouble and turmoil in our lives. Think back, if you will, to Adam and Eve. Their story represents us so well. God gives them life, puts them in a beautiful garden, and explains to them their boundaries. God also gives them the freedom to live as they choose within these boundaries. But what happens? They soon forget what God has said and decide to run the show themselves. We might say that "I did it my way" was the original sin. As a result, they end up spoiling their relationship with God, and fighting with each other—at odds with themselves and their world.

Can you understand why the decision to surrender ourselves to God is so important? Put bluntly, it is the only way we are able to gain victory over our selfishness and our compulsion to control everything and everyone around us. I have personally come to learn this the hard way. In the words of Jesus of Nazareth, we must be willing to lose our lives if we want to find them (Matt. 16:25). If we turn away from this step of self-surrender, our lives will continue to be marked by those painful things that happen when we refuse to change and always want to be in charge. Let us explore what it means to yield ourselves to God.

SURRENDERING OUR WILL AND LIFE

I can still remember when I first gave myself to God. I was sixteen, wondering what life was all about and desperately looking for something that would give my life a sense of direction and purpose. It was late at night, and I was walking down Havelock Street in Port Elizabeth. Just a few days before, a close school friend whose God-committed life had impressed me deeply, had told me about the Cross. He had explained to me that the crucifixion was God's way of showing me how much I mattered. I took my friend's words seriously. Looking into the night sky, I remember saying something like this: "God, thank you for your love that I see on the Cross. I give my life to you. Please come into my life and do whatever you want with me."

It was a profoundly significant moment for me. I did not see flashing lights, or hear voices, or feel goose bumps. But, from that moment on, I knew that in some deep way I had become different. No longer did I want to be at the center of my own life. I really wanted God to be God in my life. At that time, I had no clear idea of what this choice would mean or where it would lead me. But I was willing to take that risk. Certainly it is a decision that I have never regretted.

It has been thirty-eight years now since that eventful evening. During these years I have learned so much more about what it means to really surrender myself to God's will. Here are some of the things that I had to discover, sometimes through much heartache and pain:

■ *Surrender is both a definite decision and a lifelong process that happens day by day.* It starts when we consciously decide to hand over our will and life to God. But it does not end there. It is never a one-shot experience. Each new day we will need to renew our act of surrender and offer ourselves to God again. Shifting from a self-centered lifestyle to a God-centered one takes a lifetime.

■ *Surrender involves saying yes to what God wants in every area of our lives.* To be sure, almost every day we will be confronted with those parts of ourselves that will resist this, and we will want to go back to being in charge. During these moments we need to ask God to make us willing to change, remembering all the time that we are seeking progress in our spiritual journey, rather than perfection.

■ *Surrender is a persistent struggle.* We can sincerely hand our whole lives over to God first thing in the morning, but an hour later find ourselves sick with worry about some aspect of our work or about our finances or about the future of our country. All we can do when this happens is to ask for the courage to accept what we cannot change and to change those things we can and must. Sometimes we may need to do this repeatedly throughout the day.

■ *Surrender does not mean that we abdicate our ability to respond to life's difficulties and challenges.* Nor does it mean becoming passive or inactive or passing on responsibility for our actions to God. On the contrary, when we give ourselves to God, we are empowered to take responsibility for our lives in a new way and become more proactive in doing what needs to be done. As my good friend Dallas Willard likes to say, the strongest human will is always the one that has been surrendered to God's will and acts in harmony with it.[2]

Have you perhaps caught a glimpse of what surrender could look like? It begins with a deliberate and definite decision to hand our will and life over to God. It continues as a daily process during which we seek (and sometimes struggle) to find and do God's will. Rather than turning us into passive spectators of life, surrender empowers us to live more responsibly and creatively than ever before.

This leads us to the second part of the Third Step, which suggests that we must have some basic idea of what God is like if we are going to be able to entrust ourselves to God.

A GOD WHO CARES

In his book *The Secret Life of the Soul*, Keith Miller tells this story:

A little boy was drawing a picture with intense concentration. His mother asked, "What are you drawing?"

"I am drawing a picture of God," the little boy said.

With a concerned look on her face, the mother replied, "But you can't draw a picture of God. No one knows what God looks like."

Without looking up, the boy continued drawing and replied confidently, "Well, they will when I've finished the picture."[3]

Have you ever stopped to think honestly about your picture of God? If we are going to place our lives in God's hands, we need to give some thought to what kind of hands they are. Are they safe hands? trustworthy hands? Or will they drop us? These questions are vitally important. As I pointed out in the last chapter, many people tend to see God as a heavenly tyrant, always waiting to pounce on us. When things go wrong, these folk will often say something like, "God must have it in for me." It is very difficult to give ourselves wholeheartedly to such a fickle and vengeful deity. For this reason alone, we'll do well to think about what our understanding of God is like.

Perhaps you can start right now. For a few moments, put this book aside and think about how you see God. Try to be as honest as you can. Do you believe God really cares about you, or is your God indifferent? Are you scared of God? When life goes wrong, do you assume that God is punishing you? As you reflect on these questions, note any negative feelings about your understanding of God. How do they affect your willingness to surrender yourself to God? Does your picture of God help you to trust God? Or does it make you want to keep God at a distance?

Certainly, if we are going to surrender ourselves to God, we need to be sure that God really does care for us. Indeed, the Twelve Step program points us toward just such a God. Remember the Second Step. Do you recall its invitation to believe in a Higher Power who could restore our lives to sanity? Only a genuinely loving God would be committed to making us whole again like this. Those who wrote those words had discovered from their own experience that this was what God was like, and they wanted to share this exciting discovery with us. That is why, when we come to the Third Step, they urge us to turn our life and will over to the *care of God*.

Now, I realize that as you read these words you may find it very hard to believe that God really loves you and cares about you personally. The thought that God wants to restore your life may sound too good to be true. And why, with so many millions of people to look after, should God bother about your miserable life? If you do struggle with this incredible news, I want to make a simple suggestion. Please take a long look at the Cross. This is the one place where you and I can actually get a glimpse into God's heart. The crucified, bleeding hands of Jesus remind us that no matter who we are or what we have done we are loved with a love that will never let us go. These are hands we can trust and into which we can surrender our lives with confidence.

INTO ACTION

Has decision time arrived for you? For many people the spiritual journey stops with Steps One and Two. They are willing to admit their weakness. They believe that there is a God who wants to help them. They may even request this help. But they are unwilling to take the next step of surrendering their lives as completely as they can to God. They would like God to help them, but they want to remain in control. This reluctance to move beyond the Second Step becomes a major obstacle to a deeper experience of the power of God.

This does not mean that we must force ourselves to take the Third Step if we do not have the desire to do so. If we cannot take this step with a free heart, it is far better to be honest with ourselves and admit our reluctance. Then we should rather ask to be made ready to give ourselves wholeheartedly to God. This slower route toward surrender may, for a time, be necessary for most of us. Perhaps, as you read these words, this is where you are. You are not in a place where you can give yourself to God freely, but you are willing to open yourself to be made willing to do so.

However, if you are ready to take Step Three, here is a simple way to do it: Kneel down and say something like, "God, thank you for your care and love for me. I give myself fully and utterly to you. Please take my life and do with it whatever you will." Or you may prefer to pray the prayer of commitment suggested in the Big Book of AA. Here is my colleague Bill Meeker's version of the prayer in modern-day English:

> God, I surrender myself to you. Do whatever you need to with my life. Help me to put it back together and build it again. Set me free from my bondage to self and other things so that I can be more open to doing your will. Help me to overcome my difficulties and to have victory, so that my new life will become a living testimony to your power, your love and your way of living. May I always do your will.

When we get up from our knees after praying this prayer, our outward circumstances will not have changed. Things will still be the same. But we will be different. We have become a different person inside. There is now a new center in our lives. No longer is "self" sitting on the throne. God has taken the rightful place. There is also a new focus in our hearts, expressed in that simple prayer: "Not my will, but yours be done" (Luke 22:42, NIV).

The most important thing in our lives from now on is for us to learn how to live God's way. Though things may look the same, we will approach them differently.

Above all, when we have taken this step, we slowly discover that it takes us through the doorway of defeat toward victory. We start to overcome those things that have been spoiling our lives and our relationships. However, for this change to happen, we must always remember that this step is just a decision. It has to be followed up with actions. These actions will be described in the next nine steps. But when we take the Third Step we make a commitment to turn our will and our life over to God's care. Now we face the challenge of having to take those practical steps that show we really do want to live according to God's will, one day at a time.

TAKING IT FURTHER IN GROUP SHARING

1. Share one way in which self-centeredness expresses itself in your life.
2. Do you find it easy or difficult to believe that God cares for you personally?
3. Did you learn anything new from this chapter about the meaning of "surrender"?
4. What is your response to the invitation to take Step Three?

STEP FOUR

*We made a searching and fearless
moral inventory of ourselves.*

Let us test and examine our ways,
and return to the Lord!
—Lamentations 3:40, rsv

DARING TO
FACE OURSELVES

Some time ago I had breakfast with a recovering alcoholic. Over eggs and bacon we talked about his tough drinking days. He told me how, when he went to work, he would take a bottle of brandy with him and, whenever he could, he would sneak the bottle from his desk drawer and take a quick sip. However, he would always leave the brown wrapping paper on the bottle. Intrigued by this little detail, I asked whether this was because he wanted to hide what he was drinking from his colleagues. "Not really," he answered quickly. "I left the paper on because I didn't want to see what I was drinking myself."

My friend's answer humorously illustrates the deep struggle we all have to be honest with ourselves. We do not find it easy to see ourselves as we really are, to acknowledge our faults, and to recognize our weaknesses. Knowing ourselves can often be quite unflattering. We are far more likely to concentrate on the sins, shortcomings, and character defects of those around us than to examine our own. Like my good friend, we sometimes prefer to live under brown wrapping paper.

The Fourth Step confronts this tendency to avoid facing ourselves. It reminds us that once we have surrendered ourselves to God we need to turn the searchlight onto our own lives. Those responsible for putting the Twelve Steps together knew well that if we want to change, we need to grow in self-understanding. They were deeply aware that while not expecting us to be perfect, God does expect us to progress and face the truth about who we are. Hence the challenge of taking Step Four, which I want to summarize in the following way:

We must face ourselves as honestly as we can.

Over the years I have learned that becoming honest with ourselves opens our lives, like few other things can, to the incredible depths of God's grace and acceptance and power. When we come before our Creator in simple honesty, there is a response on God's part that sets into motion a deep and lasting life-change. I am sure that this will be your experience too as you start out on this path of self-examination. Let us look, therefore, at what this Fourth Step involves.

A MORAL INVENTORY

The Fourth Step says that in order to look at ourselves honestly we need to make a moral inventory of our lives. I hope that the concept of an inventory is familiar to you. Anyone who has ever been involved in a business venture will know the importance of this. A business that does not know what stock it has to sell or what it needs will soon be in trouble. It won't be able to meet the customers' requests, and damaged stock could be taking up valuable shelf space. It won't be long before that business closes its doors. Thus the need for an inventory that accurately reflects all the facts about the available stock.

Let me try to explain what all this has to do with our spiritual lives. Some writers have suggested that when we commit ourselves to God, it is as if we are transferring a business with all its assets and liabilities to a new owner. Making a personal inventory helps us with this. It enables us to make a list of all those attitudes, actions, character traits, and hang-ups that are stored away in the warehouse of our life: the positive and the negative, the attractive and the unattractive, the good and the bad. When we make an inventory in this way, it shows that we are willing to place every part of our lives under the influence of God's protection and care.

Notice that the Fourth Step describes this personal check-up as a "moral" one. This seems to suggest that when we make an inventory of our lives we should look carefully at the ways in which we have done wrong. Generally speaking, this list will include those occasions on which we have acted against our better judgment, hurt and harmed others, and let ourselves down. Perhaps there will be a few other things too. I suspect that when we have completed this list it will contain many of our failures—failure to love those close to us, failure to speak the truth, failure to honor our commitments.

Our list of liabilities must also include those weaknesses described in Step One. Remember them? The character defects that reveal our self-centeredness and our need always to be in control; feelings of resentment, fear, and anger that rob us of serenity and often turn our minds into battlefields; destructive habits that continually defeat us and that we cannot seem to overcome in our own strength. In other words, it is not just our moral wrongs that need to be faced but all those other character flaws that often make our lives miserable and steal our joy.

We must, however, also be sure that we make a list of our assets. Here we include those positive qualities in our lives that we can celebrate and affirm. These might be our ability to do certain things well or character traits that bring out the best in us and enrich the lives of people around us. Some may find doing this quite difficult. They may be afraid of boasting or being arrogant. On the contrary, unless we are willing to name both our vices and our virtues, we will not end up with an accurate and balanced assessment of our lives.

SEARCHING AND FEARLESS

Strict honesty with ourselves is crucial to the experience of deep inner change. We can confirm this fact by simple observation. Consider the individuals in groups you belong to. Who is growing in his or her relationship with God? Who is finding a new joy, peace, and serenity? Who is relating more freely and openly to others? Who is winning the battle against destructive addictions like gambling, overeating, or substance abuse? These are not necessarily the people who seem very religious, who know their Bible well, or who can recite the Twelve Steps. Most likely they are people who are just trying to be as honest as they can with themselves.

It is no wonder, therefore, that the Fourth Step asks us to make a "searching" and "fearless" moral inventory. Both these adjectives are well chosen and deserve careful thought. On the one hand, we must carefully *search out* all the facts about our lives. When we make our list of assets and liabilities, we would do well to make thoroughness our checkpoint. On the other hand, we must also be *fearless*. It can sometimes be a bit scary to face ourselves with total honesty. This may be why some try to excuse themselves from the ordeal by saying something like, "Why should I go digging up all these things from the past? Let sleeping dogs lie. After all, I have taken the first three steps and surrendered myself to God. I don't need to do anything more." Few things block our spiritual progress more than excuses like these.

The journey toward a more ruthless honesty can be made easier by asking ourselves a few tough questions. The AA's Big Book says that these questions may be grouped into five areas: our resentments, our fears, our sexuality, our finances, and our social relationships.[1]

Here are some questions that I have found particularly helpful. If you later decide to take the Fourth Step, you may like to think about them as a starting point for your own attempts to get to understand yourself more honestly.

- Regarding our *resentments* we can ask: Who are the people I resent? What did they do or say to hurt me? Then, rather than dwell on their actions and words, we can ask ourselves the difficult question: What did I say or do that might have caused them to react the way they did?
- Regarding our *fears* we can ask: What fears have dominated my life since childhood? Why was I afraid in these ways? What do I fear at the moment? To help us face these fears, we always need to remember that they are not bigger than we can handle. With God as our Higher Power we are stronger than our greatest fear.
- Regarding our *sexual lives* we can ask: When and how did I harm another person sexually? Have I been sexually faithful? How do I respond when my requests for sex are denied? Do I tend to see people primarily as sex objects to be used

or abused by me for my own gratification? Have I ever withheld sex as punishment or used it as a weapon?

- Regarding our *financial affairs* we can ask: Am I extravagant? Or am I greedy, tightfisted, and selfish? Am I irresponsible with money? Do I live beyond my means? Have I tried to cut corners financially? Am I honest in my business dealings? Have I tended to make money the most important thing in my life?

- Regarding our *social relationships* we can ask: Do I insist on getting my own way by trying to dominate those around me? Do I seek to control others by having hurt feelings, by developing a sense of persecution, or by withdrawing into a sulky silence? Am I willing to contribute to the well-being of others, or am I just a taker? Do I discriminate between people on the basis of gender or color or culture?

Making an inventory along these lines emphasizes our seriousness about wanting to become honest. It shows that we are no longer prepared to deceive ourselves about who we are; nor are we going to try to rationalize away our faults and shortcomings any more and pretend to be who we are not. When we decide to set aside the time to take stock of our assets and liabilities, we are in effect saying to God, "Here is my life, warts and all, that I transfer into your safekeeping. I really do want to change and grow into the person that you want me to be. Thank you for accepting me as I am and for being willing to draw the starting line for our relationship right where I find myself at this moment."

INTO ACTION

Now is the time for you to consider moving from theory into action. Remember, *action* is always the magic word! It is not enough to have lots of head knowledge about what a personal inventory is. We actually need to walk down the aisle of our lives, clipboard and pencil in hand, and make a careful, written list of our assets and liabilities. If you are ready for this adventure in personal stocktaking, I can offer some practical guidelines.

We can begin by reminding ourselves that God is with us and wants to help us to be honest with ourselves. One way to do this is to pray the well-known words from Psalm 139:23–24, NIV.

> *Search me, O God, and know my heart;*
> *Test me and know my anxious thoughts.*
> *See if there is any offensive way in me,*
> *and lead me in the way everlasting.*

Next, using the questions given earlier in the chapter, we can make specific notes about our resentments and envies, our fears and angers, our lusts and greed, our possessiveness and struggles to let go. We can then also list those character defects and shortcomings that cause us much trouble and turmoil. When I did this for the first time many years ago, I can remember listing things like "not telling the whole truth," "always wanting to be in the right," "withdrawing from loved ones when things do not go my own way," and a host of other self-centered and controlling behaviors. It was not easy to write these things down in black and white, but once I had done so, I felt as if I had been set free and was able to relax more than I had done in a long time.

We must not forget to place a positive list of our assets along-side our list of liabilities. If we focus only on the negative, we end up with a lopsided view of who we are. When we name our good qualities and the things we do well, we gain a far more realistic perspective on our lives. We are able to see that, while we are most certainly flawed and imperfect human beings with very definite limitations, we can also become so much more than we are at the moment. Getting our strengths down on paper like this puts us in touch with our own exciting potential.

The last thing we must remember when we take this step is that daring to know ourselves is an ongoing and never-ending process. We will not understand everything about ourselves after one try at making a personal inventory. There will always be more things to discover. For this reason it has been rightly stated that Step Four is simply the beginning of a lifetime habit of self-examination and personal reflection for those who want to grow and change. Nonetheless, it all begins when we decide to take off the brown wrapping paper!

TAKING IT FURTHER IN GROUP SHARING

1. Why do you think we find it difficult to be honest with ourselves?
2. What is your response to the idea of a "moral inventory"?
3. Share one asset that you would list in your moral inventory.
4. What is your response to the invitation to take Step Four?

STEP FIVE

*We admitted to God, to ourselves,
and to another human being the
exact nature of our wrongs.*

Therefore confess your sins to one another,
and pray for one another, so that you may
be healed.

—James 5:16

COMING CLEAN

One Sunday I preached about confession and extended an invitation. If anyone wanted to confess, he or she could come to the chapel the following Tuesday evening between six and seven o'clock. Not being part of a church that normally does this kind of thing, I didn't expect many people to come. I was wrong. Over thirty people turned up. After spending time with each one personally, I finally left the chapel near midnight.

I was deeply moved by what had happened. I knew it had taken a lot of courage for those who came to share their shortcomings and defects. I felt it a sacred privilege to be allowed into those rooms of their lives that had been locked up for years. Fresh winds of relief and release began to blow where once there had been only stale air of guilt and remorse. People seemed to leave with a lighter and more joyful step than when they had walked in. One person told me afterward, "It took a long time to get around to doing this, but I am so glad I did."

I am telling you this because the Fifth Step can be seen as a form of confession. But it is also something more. It is a time for coming out of hiding, sharing our secrets, bringing the skeletons out of the cupboard, taking off our masks, and finding new freedom and peace. Here is how I like to summarize it:

We must come clean to the best of our ability.

Even though this step sounds very daunting, most of us would agree that coming clean is a positive thing. The wisdom of taking this step is underlined by the biblical writer who, long before the beginning of Alcoholics Anonymous, wrote, "Confess your sins to one another, and pray for one another, so that you may be healed" (James 5:16). Today psychiatrists, psychologists, and other mental health professionals point out the deep need in all of us to speak about the hidden things in our lives. So let's see what it may mean for us to put the Fifth Step into practice.

ADMITTING OUR WRONGS

The Fifth Step has three parts. First of all, it says that *we must admit our wrongs to God.* We can do this very simply. We come before God with our list of failures and sins and say something like, "Lord, here I am. I do not want to hide anything from you. I bring you the story of my wrongdoing. Thank you that you accept me as I am. Please forgive me and help me to change." Making our confession along these lines reopens the channels between God and ourselves. We discover the cleansing power of God's mercy flowing deeply into our lives. The way is prepared for us to make a new beginning.

Second, *we must admit our wrongs to ourselves.* This means looking at our moral inventory again and acknowledging, "This is who I am. There are no excuses for what I have done. I am not going to blame my upbringing, my genes, or my circumstances. These actions and words are not the result of what others have done or not done to me. I take the blame. I am willing to take full responsibility for them." When we are willing to face ourselves honestly in this way, we open the way for positive change to take place in our lives.

Third, *we must admit our wrongs to one other human being.* This is the scary part of the Fifth Step. We don't want anyone else to know about our shameful past. We prefer that people think of us as virtuous, well-meaning, and good. Anything that may contradict this larger-than-life image of ourselves must be stored away in the basement of our lives, out of public view. We would much rather remain in hiding, have our secrets go to the grave with us, chain up the ghosts of the past, and keep our masks firmly in place than come clean in the presence of another human being.

I know this resistance only too well. I put off doing the Fifth Step for several years. I would keep saying to myself, "I have already confessed all my wrongdoing to God. I have received God's forgiveness. I have acknowledged my responsibility for my bad choices. I do not need to go through the whole process again with another human being. Besides, I'm not a Catholic, and this confession thing is not part of my tradition." Perhaps you can identify with one or another of these excuses.

But we avoid this part of Step Five to our detriment. Let me describe some of the enormous spiritual and emotional benefits of coming clean. Once we become aware of what we could receive as a result of admitting our wrongs, we may be keener to take this difficult step for ourselves.

SOME BENEFITS

As you read through these benefits, please know that I have not simply made them up. They come from my many conversations with recovering alcoholics and others who have taken this step.

They are also part of my own experience. Here are four blessings that you can receive when you admit your wrongs to God, yourself, *and* one other human being.

A stronger self-worth

We seldom feel good about ourselves when we do wrong. Just think about your own experience. Try a quick exercise. Think back to the last time you lied to a loved one, betrayed a confidence, gossiped behind a colleague's back, or treated someone unfairly. Let me ask you: Did your behavior in this instance make you feel better? Did it increase or diminish your sense of worth? My guess is that it made it harder for you to respect yourself as you should. Certainly this is what happens to me when I hurt or harm someone else.

Doing the Fifth Step, however, helps us to regain our sense of self-worth. Those who come clean know that they have done a remarkably brave thing. They have had the courage not only to be honest with God and themselves about their wrongdoing, but also to make a confession to a trusted person. They can rightly congratulate themselves for doing this. Thinking back to my own experience, I can remember clearly how good I felt about myself when I took this step.

Release from guilt

As a result of doing things that go against what we know to be right and true, nearly all of us carry some kind of guilt with us. Some people tell us that we should not feel guilty at all about our deeds of selfishness and anger and prejudice. I disagree! Guilt shows that we have at least some moral awareness of what is right and wrong. But what is even more important is how we respond to our guilt. Will it motivate us to change and try to become better persons, or will we allow it to make us spiritually, emotionally, and perhaps even physically sick? In the end everything depends on the way we decide to deal with it.

The only remedy for guilt that we can really trust is God's free offer of forgiveness. We call this "God's grace." Amazing grace! Nothing else has the power to release us more completely from our guilt than this gift. However, we have to experience it for ourselves. It is not enough just to know about it in our minds. This is where the Fifth Step can be so powerful. When we are able to be open about the very worst in ourselves and to experience the acceptance of another human being, it so often makes the forgiveness of God personally real to us. We actually *feel* relieved from the burden of our guilt.

Deeper relationships

When we keep our shameful deeds hidden, we often cut ourselves off from others and hurt our relationships. We assume that if others really knew the truth about what we have done, they would have nothing to do with us. Our relationships tend to become superficial and often get messed up. Sometimes we even believe that no one else could be as bad as we are. Small wonder that our unconfessed wrongs so often cause us to isolate ourselves from those around us. A man who had walked a few miles down the AA road commented that our secrets can make us feel very lonely.

Coming clean breaks this awful sense of isolation. When someone who cares listens to us talking about those things that weigh heavily on our conscience and doesn't reject us, it restores our sense of human belonging. We don't feel as lonely as we once did. We realize that we are not the only ones who have sinned or failed. Having taken this step to come clean with an understanding friend, we experience again a deeper connection with others.

Genuine spirituality

A common criticism often thrown at religious people is that they are not sincere. The word usually used is *hypocrite*. As someone who works in a church, I accept this criticism. I have not always been honest and open about myself. Too often I have given the impression of being a better person than I really am. I do not admit this lightly. The Bible repeatedly points out that one of the biggest obstacles in our relationship with God revolves around this tendency to pretend to be what we are not. Think, for example, of the many times Jesus speaks out against the hypocrisy of the religious leaders of his day.

We discover a far more genuine spirituality when we come clean. We find out that it is precisely where we have most deeply failed that we most deeply experience the love and power of God. As we face up to our wrongdoing, we become less condemning and more understanding of others who have failed. Perhaps most significantly, when we are prepared to admit our own imperfections, we begin to live with a freer spirit and a lighter heart. We begin to have a relationship with God in which we are able to be who we really are—flawed, limited, and fallible human beings, always in need of God's help and mercy.

INTO ACTION

Let me tell you about my own first Fifth Step experience. Over twenty years ago I phoned an elderly priest and explained what I needed to do. We made an appointment to meet. When I arrived, he took me into a small chapel. I knelt down before a wooden crucifix and read aloud the moral inventory that I had written down. Then my companion asked a few questions. Some things I had said needed further exploration, in some relationships I needed to make amends, and in others I needed to ask for forgiveness. When he had finished speaking, the priest did something I have never forgotten. He took my notes, tore them up, and threw the pieces into a wastepaper basket. He ended our time with a simple prayer in which he thanked God for the gift of forgiveness and the possibility of new beginnings.

I share my story, not because it is the only way to take this step, but because it highlights some of the main things involved. To begin with, we need to choose the person with whom we would be happy to take this step very carefully. It must be someone who is trustworthy, understanding, and able to keep confidences. He or she could be a minister or a priest, a doctor or a psychologist, a mentor or a close friend. Or it could be someone we don't know too well but who really understands what we are doing. Preferably it should be someone of the same gender who will not be harmed or compromised in any way by what we have to share.

Then we need to contact this person and set a time to meet. We will need to explain that we are doing the Twelve Step program and that part of the process is to come clean with another human being. The Big Book of AA reminds us that most people approached in this way will be only too glad to help and more often than not will be honored by our confidence in them.

Our next responsibility will be to prepare ourselves for the meeting. If we did Step Four thoroughly, most of this preparation will already have been done. It always helps to have our written moral inventory with us when we see the person we have chosen. Not only will it keep us from straying into generalities; it will also help us overcome any nervousness or doubt we may feel.

Lastly, we need to be as fearless and thorough as we possibly can in our sharing. Often the things we most need to speak about will be the ones we find hardest to say. In the end there may be some things that we just cannot bring ourselves to reveal. All that we can do then is to say, "There are some things that I haven't spoken about yet and which I may bring into the open sometime in the future." We do not need to get everything right when we do this step. As always, we should remember that we are seeking to make progress in our spiritual journey and not to arrive at perfection in a single moment.

I wonder how you are feeling about Step Five at the moment. I would not be surprised if you are experiencing a great deal of resistance or at least mixed emotions. Most Twelve Steppers will tell you that this was the one step they most wanted to avoid in the program. So if you are afraid, be gentle with yourself. Know that you are not alone in your fear. However, let me say again: if others have been able to take this step and experience the wonderful peace that it brings, you can too.

TAKING IT FURTHER IN GROUP SHARING

1. Why do you think we find it hard to "come clean"?
2. Have you ever experienced the benefits of confession? If so, could you share one of them?
3. How do you think the practice of confession can be misused?
4. What is your response to the invitation to take Step Five?

STEP SIX

We were entirely ready to have God remove all these defects of character.

I appeal to you therefore, brothers and sisters, by the mercies of God, to present your bodies as a living sacrifice. . . . Do not be conformed to this world, but be transformed by the renewing of your minds, so that you may discern what is the will of God—what is good and acceptable and perfect.

—Romans 12:1–2

READY AND WILLING

Have you heard the story of the little boy who was standing, trembling, while his father read over the poor school report card that he had just brought home? His father read aloud one bad grade after another, his frown deepening all the time. Finally, to break the awkward tension, the little boy said, "Dad, what do you think my trouble is, environment or heredity?"

The boy's query raises several questions about where our character defects come from. Are they the result of the environment in which we have grown up? Are they the consequence of inherited chromosomes? Or are they a mixture of both? Many people would give one of these answers. But might not other factors be involved as well? Could they be the product of how we ourselves have chosen to think and behave? These questions are not merely academic. Our response to them will strongly affect how we go about making changes in our lives.

We have all been conditioned for better or for worse by our upbringing, by the surrounding society, and by our biological genes. There can be little doubt about this. But it is equally true that what distinguishes us human beings from the rest of creation is our ability to choose what kind of person we want to become. We can stay as we are if we want, or we can decide to move toward becoming the person we believe we are meant to be. The choice is ours. Think of the many times in the Bible that people are invited to choose a new direction for their lives.

Let's face facts, though. Is there not perhaps another reason why we like to blame our circumstances and our genes for our negative traits? Could it be that we simply do not want to face the challenge involved in personal change? Maybe our character flaws have become such a part of our makeup that we don't know how we would live without them. It could be that we even enjoy them! We might actually like feeling superior or having a grandiose image of ourselves or controlling others and always trying to get our way. The thought of getting rid of these things might not be attractive at all.

For the moment, I am going to assume that you really are sincere about dealing with your character defects. When we work through the first five steps they often help us to recognize our need for change. We start believing that it may be worth the trouble of letting God help transform us into more loving, more honest, and less self-centered human beings. The burning question that faces us is: how do we facilitate these deep changes in our character?

This is where the wisdom of the Sixth Step can guide us. It describes the attitude that we need to develop if we want to experience personal change. Here is my description of this attitude:

We must be ready to surrender all our character flaws
and be willing to let God change us.

Developing this attitude has two distinct parts to it. Let us take a closer look.

BEING ENTIRELY READY

First of all, we must be entirely ready to let go of all our character flaws. This does not mean that we think we are suddenly going to become perfect. Far from it! Even Paul, the author of many New Testament letters, battled with his weaknesses until he died.[1] It goes without saying that to be human is to be imperfect. We grow and mature throughout our lives. But what this attitude of complete readiness does indicate is that we are fully prepared to give up any destructive pattern of thought or behavior that is stopping our spiritual progress. We are open to the total renewal of our lives.

A simple picture underlines the crucial importance of this attitude. What is the first thing we need to do if we want to buy a new car? Some may say that we need to go to the local car dealership or begin looking in the motor vehicle section of the daily newspapers to see which cars are for sale. However, that is not really what comes first. Right at the outset, we need to be entirely ready to give up driving the old car. Only then will we be able to start out on the journey towards changing cars.

It is exactly the same when it comes to wanting to change ourselves. We must be completely prepared to give up parts of the person we once were. If this challenge sounds too demanding, there are a number of ways in which we can encourage ourselves to have this attitude of entire readiness. Here are some you might like to consider:

■ *We can picture our life as we believe God wants it to be.* For example, we can think about what is known in the Bible as the "fruit of the Spirit" growing within us. We can imagine ourselves filled with goodness, love, joy, peace, patience, kindness, faithfulness, gentleness, and self-control. Would we not like to be a person like that?

■ *We can think about what our lives would be like if we don't let go of our character defects.* At the very least, it will mean that we are going to stay the same as we are until we die— that we do not want to become a better person in any way. What a soul-destroying thought!

■ *We can think about the pain that our character defects have caused others and ourselves.* They may have ruined our family relationships, cost us a promotion, lost us our jobs, made us drink heavily, gotten us into trouble, or even made us ill. The one good thing about these painful consequences is that they can bring us to the point where we say, "I cannot go on living like this. I need to change."

■ *We can ask God to help us to develop a greater readiness for change.* As we have seen, there may be some character flaws that we want to keep. In this case, the most honest thing for us to do would be to admit our reluctance and pray something like this, "Lord, I honestly don't want to let go of all my character defects just yet. Please help me to change this attitude."

Before you read further, I invite you to put this book down for a few minutes and to try out one or two of these suggestions. See whether they encourage you to become more open to giving up all your shortcomings and character flaws. My hunch is that they will.

BEING WILLING TO LET
GOD CHANGE US

Second, we must be open to letting God change us. Inner change is not just a do-it-yourself job. We all know what usually happens when we grit our teeth, clench our knuckles, and try to change ourselves through our own efforts. We come up short. While there might be some outward changes for a brief time, before long our true character shows itself again. We need some kind of power from outside ourselves. As the Alcoholics Anonymous slogan puts it, "I can't, God can. Let Him."

The wonderful news is that God actually wants to help us become better persons. Let's go back to Step Two again. Do you remember what it said? There is a Higher Power available to each one of us. No matter who we are, or what we have done, or where we have been, this Higher Power accepts us, cares about us, and longs to make it possible for us to become a new person. We don't have to go it all on our own. There is Someone who deeply wants to come alongside us as we seek to replace our character flaws with more positive behavior.

The main reason we need God and a power from outside ourselves is that real change always flows from inside us. It comes from the heart. It is not something external or superficial. We cannot reach inside ourselves and pull out the roots of our own character failings. It is God's Spirit alone that can do this inner work. This is our deepest need. When we are willing to let God do this, it is literally as if a heavy load has been lifted from our shoulders.

Let me say immediately that this does not mean that we are invited to sit back and do nothing. There is also a need for carefully planned effort on our own part, as long as we don't try to do what only God can do. What we can do, and must do, is to work through the Twelve Steps. They can put our lives in the way of God's transforming love and power like few other things can. And at this stage of the program it means that we are ready to give up all our character defects and are willing to let God change us.

It may be helpful to visualize this division of labor between God and ourselves. Picture a narrow ledge with a sheer drop on either side. The chasm on the right is the danger that we fall into when we try to change by our own efforts. The chasm on the left is the danger of sitting back and doing nothing. On the ledge there is a narrow path—a path that leads to personal change and inner transformation. It is the path of cooperation with God—of being ready to give up all our character defects and being willing to let God change us. We must veer off neither to the left nor to the right, but we must stay on the path. When we do, the power of God will bring change to us from the inside out.[2]

Are you ready to walk along this narrow pathway?

INTO ACTION

Cultivating this new attitude of readiness and willingness may not seem like work, but it is. It involves much thinking, reflecting, praying, and doing. Here is an exercise in which you can use these four activities to help you make progress with this step.

Look at this list of some common character defects. Think about them slowly. Reflect on how each one expresses itself in our lives, and then check off the ones you personally struggle with (or enjoy!).

Defensiveness	Laziness	False pride
Lust	Procrastination	Overspending
Impatience	Overpromising	Prejudice
Gluttony	Resentment	Hypercriticalness
Touchiness	Rationalization	Perfectionism
Unreliability	Manipulation	Worry
Self-pity	Phoniness	Greed
Self-centeredness	Irresponsibility	Ungratefulness
Smugness	Gossip	Self-righteousness
Indifference	Dishonesty	Anger
Apathy	Blaming others	Racism
Suspicion	Envy	Control

Once you have ticked off those defects that describe your own life, go back to each one and spend some time thinking more deeply about it. Think of the different ways in which you have tried to fix yourself in the past with regard to this particular character defect. Let's say you've always struggled with impatience. How have you tried in vain to change this trait? Perhaps you put notes on the fridge reminding yourself to be more patient, read Bible verses on the subject, or repeat affirmations like, "I see myself as a patient person." Do not let all these failed efforts depress you. Rather ask yourself, "Am I ready to give up this character defect and open to let God change me?" If your answer is yes, then you are in the process of taking the Sixth Step.

You might like to finish the exercise by saying or writing out a short, simple prayer that expresses your readiness and willingness to change. It could go something like this:

"Dear God, it is a great relief to realize that I don't have to try to change myself in my own strength. Thank you for wanting to help me. I'm ready now to give you all my character defects and willing for you to change me in whatever way you want. Amen."

How did it go? If we are prepared to take this step, we are saying that we want something better for our lives. We want to become the best that we can be. We want to make God's dream for our lives a reality. We want to grow into our full potential for becoming a loving and caring person, for, as a poster once proclaimed, "Who we are is God's gift to us. Who we become is our gift to God."

TAKING IT FURTHER IN GROUP SHARING

1. Why do you think we sometimes struggle to let go of our character flaws and defects?
2. Share one character defect that you would like to see changed in your own life.
3. How would you describe the division of labor between God and ourselves when it comes to the issue of inner change?
4. What is your response to the invitation to take Step Six?

STEP SEVEN

We humbly asked God to remove our shortcomings.

Humble yourselves before the Lord and he will exalt you.

—James 4:10, RSV

THE QUEST
FOR HUMILITY

How are you finding the Twelve Step program so far? As we reach the halfway mark, it may help to recap briefly our journey to this point. During the first six steps we admitted our weaknesses, affirmed the availability of a caring Higher Power, surrendered ourselves to God, dared to examine ourselves as honestly as we could, came clean, and became ready and willing for God to remove all our character defects. If you have taken these steps, I am sure that you have already begun to experience a greater freedom, serenity, and spiritual awareness.

We come now to what has been called the spiritual watershed moment of the program.[1] Although the Seventh Step sounds simple and straightforward, its importance cannot be stressed too strongly. Taking this step turns our lives in a completely new direction. It makes it clear that we do not want to continue with our past destructive attitudes and patterns of behavior. We really want to become different people. It also underlines again that this inner change is mainly God's work and not ours. Here is the way I like to explain this step:

We must be humble enough to ask God to help us change into the people God wants us to be.

This step introduces us to a vitally important principle of the spiritual world—the principle of asking. The Bible constantly stresses this. If we want God to work in our lives, we must ask.[2] In order to change us, God must have our cooperation. Unless we make it clear to God that we really do want our character flaws removed, it's highly unlikely that God will just barge in and do so automatically. To experience God's transforming power, we must have the courage to ask for it.

However, learning to ask in the right way requires humility. Children teach us this truth. Have you noticed? They are not too proud to ask for what they need. They just stretch out their hands and ask. Small wonder Jesus once said that if we want to enter more fully into God's love and power we need to humble ourselves and become like children (Matt. 18:2-3). So let's take a closer look at this step's importance for those who want to change.

HUMBLY ASK

In his book *The Ragamuffin Gospel*, Brennan Manning tells a story along these lines:

> A man sat across the desk from his doctor and complained, "Doctor, I have an awful headache. Can you help me to get rid of it?"
>
> "Certainly," answered the doctor. "But I need to ask a few questions first. Tell me, do you drink at all?"
>
> "Alcohol!" said the man, "I don't touch the stuff."
>
> "Do you smoke at all?"

"Tobacco is disgusting! I've never smoked a cigarette in my life."

"I'm a bit embarrassed to ask you this, but it's important. Do you run around with other women besides your wife?"

"Of course I don't, Doctor. Who do you think I am? I'm in bed every night by ten at the latest."

"Tell me," asked the doctor, "that pain in your head—is it a sharp shooting pain?"

"Yes," said the man. "It's a sharp shooting pain."

"Well, I know what is causing it. Your trouble is that you have your halo on too tight. You need to loosen it a bit."[3]

People laugh when I retell this story. They obviously find it amusing. Another reason for their laughter, I suspect, could be that they recognize something about themselves in it. Certainly I do. How often do we give the impression that we are more honest, more caring, more virtuous than we really are? While in theory we may be willing to admit to our faults, we often become defensive when anyone reminds us of them. A quick test: how did you respond the last time someone pointed out one of your character flaws?

True humility involves loosening our halos. It's about becoming honest with ourselves, acknowledging both our strengths and our weaknesses, accepting that we can be both saint and sinner, angel and monster. It's about seeing ourselves as we really are. Humility neither exaggerates nor plays down the truth about who we are. It simply accepts the reality that we are fragile, flawed, and fallible human beings who need a power beyond ourselves if we are going to become the people God wants us to be. In short, this is what it means to be humble: being real about who we are.

Can you see more clearly now why the Seventh Step requires humility? Without humility there can be little honest prayer. We will just be mouthing empty, lifeless clichés that have little connection with our real needs. By contrast, humble people know how messed up their lives really are. They are ready and willing to call out to God for help. Asking God to help them change comes naturally, and God's power can start working to make them whole. The Bible says bluntly: "God opposes the proud, but gives grace to the humble" (1 Pet. 5:5, RSV).

BECOMING HUMBLE

How do we gain a greater measure of humility? This is a tricky question. Ironically, seeking a deeper humility without becoming proud can be difficult. What often happens is this: As we try to become humble, we start comparing ourselves with those around us. We think to ourselves that others are not quite as humble as they should be. Worse still, they are not as humble as we are. Before we know it, we find ourselves arriving at a totally different destination than the one we originally had in our sights. Whereas we were aiming to become humbler, the end result is that we have become more humbly proud!

The best recipe for humility I know of was put together by a dear friend whom I deeply respect. It has been a great challenge to me.[4] The fact that I share it does not mean that I have mastered it—far from it. Nonetheless, it does give us some practical ways we can open our lives to the gift of humility. It suggests that besides waiting for God to act in our lives we need to commit ourselves to stop doing three things:

- *We need to stop pretending to be what we know we are not.* At some point in our growing-up years we make the powerful discovery that we can manipulate the truth about ourselves in order to look good. More simply put, we learn how to pretend. If we feel inadequate, we can pretend to be self-sufficient. If we are sad, we can put on a happy face. If life is falling apart, we can look as if we have everything together. Giving up these attempts at pretending puts our feet firmly on the path toward a truer humility.

- *We need to stop presuming that we are more important than other people.* One way in which we can do this is by disciplining ourselves to serve others quietly, without applause. Opportunities for quiet service present themselves every day. We could give a colleague a lift. We could take an interest in those who cannot enhance our status or reputation. We might take the garbage can out without being asked! These small acts of service go a long way in helping us conquer our tendency toward pride and self-importance.

- *We need to stop pushing our will onto others.* In Step Three we looked at our deep-seated instinct to be controlling and to play the part of God ourselves. We often tend to do this in our close relationships. Think of how we try to straighten out others, fix them with our solutions, or get them to do what we want them to do. It can be quite humbling to realize that only God actually knows what is best for those around us. The best that we can do, most of the time, is just to be there for them, to listen to what they are going through, and perhaps to ask some questions that could help them know what to do next.

Let me try to summarize this a little more positively. If we want to cook up some humility, we need to mix three basic ingredients: We need to be ourselves, to serve others, and to let God be God. Then we add daily measures of prayer, honest sharing, and a deep surrender to God's Spirit. Allow to simmer for as long as necessary. Do not keep lifting the lid to examine what is happening. One day we will find ourselves surprised by the aroma of God's grace and power at work in our lives!

The strange thing about humility is that there is something paradoxical about it. When we think we've got it, we are usually furthest from it. Those who possess it do not realize that they are humble. In the end, it is really a gift that God gives us and works in us. We cannot achieve it ourselves, manufacture it, or earn it; we can simply open our hands and hearts to receive it.

INTO ACTION

The essential action involved in this step is prayer. Prayer is simply asking God to remove our shortcomings. This is how those in Alcoholics Anonymous often express this desire. You may like to make this prayer your own:

> *My Creator, I am now willing that you should have all of me, good and bad. I pray that you now remove from me every single defect of character which stands in the way of my usefulness to you and my fellows. Grant me strength, as I go out from here, to do your bidding. Amen.*[5]

Now, it is very unlikely that when we pray this prayer all our character flaws will suddenly disappear. Why is this? Has God not heard our prayer? Do we not pray with enough faith? Should we keep on praying? How are we to expect God to answer this prayer? Our responses to these questions will have a strong bearing on the way we go about taking this step. Here are some thoughts that come out of my own experience.

First of all, inner change is often an uneven, up-and-down process. It hardly ever happens instantly or in a neat and orderly way. It cannot be charted on a graph as a straight line going steadily upward. In fact, spiritual growth usually involves taking three steps forward and two back! The line on the graph goes up, down, and sideways, giving it a rather topsy-turvy shape. Just when we think we have overcome some fault, it reappears under a different guise and we've got to deal with it again.

This leads me to a second thought about change. When a character defect shows up again, we need to go back and ask God again to help us to conquer it. In my book *The Serenity Prayer* I used the picture of an elevator going up to God to illustrate this point. Whenever we find ourselves struggling with a particular fault, for example, when we always want to be in the right, we need to imagine ourselves picking up that fault as if it were a poisonous snake. We then place it in a sack and put it on the elevator. If the sack comes back again, as it surely will, we can have a quick look inside, check what it is, and place it back on the elevator immediately. Then we can get on with doing whatever we need to. But don't try to beat the character defect in your own strength. If you do, it will get the better of you each time. Each time it returns, simply put it back on the elevator. After days or perhaps weeks, months, or even years, we will notice one day that it hasn't come back. And we will know that God is busy changing us—making us new.

The third thought goes like this: when we ask God to remove our character flaws, we also need to actively replace them with the opposite qualities. If we battle with selfishness, we can begin to do kind or helpful things for others. If we procrastinate a lot, we can get down to doing something that we have been avoiding. As we take action to build positive habits like these into our lives with God's help, our prayers for change will become more effective. After all, as the Bible makes very clear, faith without works is dead (James 2:17).

I close this chapter with a prayer that I heard some years ago: "O God, I ain't what I could be, and I ain't what I should be, but, thanks be to you, I ain't what I used to be!" These words summarize what we can expect to happen when we apply Step Seven on a regular basis. We may always be flawed, imperfect, in progress, on the way. But when we become humble enough to ask God to remove our character defects, God will start changing us, one day at a time, into the people God wants us to be.

TAKING IT FURTHER IN GROUP SHARING

1. How do you respond when you hear the word *humility?*
2. Do you find it easy or difficult to ask for what you need?
3. What do you think about the recipe for humility mentioned in this chapter?
4. What is your response to the invitation to take Step Seven?

STEP EIGHT

*We made a list of all persons we
had harmed, and became willing
to make amends to them all.*

Those who say, "I love God," and hate their brothers or sisters, are liars; for those who do not love
a brother or sister whom they have seen, cannot
love God whom they have not seen. . . . those who
love God must love their brothers and sisters also.
—1 John 4:20–21

CHAPTER EIGHT

REFLECTING ON OUR RELATIONSHIPS

Once I took part in a group discussion on the question: in which area of life have you failed the most? My answer was not long in coming. It was not in the academic arena or the sporting, the vocational or the financial. While I have certainly blown it more than once in each of these areas, they are not my biggest failures. My biggest failures have been in my relationships. I cannot believe how many times I have let down my family, my friends, and my colleagues through what I have done or failed to do.

I remember one painful moment in my marriage. It was some twenty years ago. I had just taken responsibility for my first congregation. Obviously keen to succeed, I worked long, hard hours. Outwardly things were going well. Attendance was growing; finances had improved; and a new sanctuary was on the drawing board. But in my marriage I was not doing well at all. I was often away from home or out late. I was denying the person closest to me the attention, time, and energy necessary for real communication and caring. I came home one night to find on my bedside table a note that read: "Trevor, I love you and want to be married to you. I sometimes worry, though, that one day I may no longer be worried if you don't come home. I miss you and want to reconnect. Debbie."

Have you experienced similar moments of failure in your relationships? I'm sure you have. Let me tell you why. Remember those character flaws that we looked at earlier? They don't harm only us; they harm others as well. It could be our desire to be in control; our explosive temper; our selfishness; our long-held resentments; our not speaking the truth; our deep-seated prejudices; our wanting everything perfect around us; or, as was the case in my marriage, our tendency to overcommit ourselves and take on too much. But regardless of the shape they take, our faults and failures always damage our lives and the lives of those closest to us.

This social aspect of our character flaws has one important implication. It is this: if we want to progress along the spiritual path, we have to deal with the harm that we have caused other people. This will mean acknowledging our broken and bruised relationships, taking responsibility for the part we have played in them, and making whatever amends are necessary. Step Eight begins this process of reflecting on our relationships. Here is how I understand it:

> *We must accept that we have hurt others and be willing to make restitution.*

There are strong biblical reasons for taking this step. The New Testament writers were convinced that it is almost impossible to grow spiritually if we do not do something about the ways in which we have harmed others. They understood that we cannot have one posture toward God and another toward people. We cannot, for example, say that we want to grow closer to God, yet remain closed off to our brother or sister. As the apostle John once wrote, "For those who do not love a brother or sister whom they have seen, cannot love God whom they have not seen" (1 John 4:20).

Let us therefore look a little more closely at how this step prepares us to care for those around us better—at home, in our places of work and worship, and in the community.

REMEMBERING THOSE WE HAVE HARMED

The first part of the Eighth Step asks us to make a list of those we have harmed. This challenge is a continuation of the journey we began in the Fourth Step. There we looked mainly at ourselves. We made a written inventory of our strengths and weaknesses, our assets and liabilities. Now we are being asked to turn the spotlight on our relationships. In effect, this step says to us: reflect on your relationships. Remember the faces of those you have hurt. Write down their names. Think carefully about what it was that you did or did not do that harmed them.

This will be a difficult task for most of us. When things go wrong in our relationships, we don't usually respond in this way. In fact, our initial reaction is often exactly the opposite. We want to justify ourselves. We become defensive. We insist that we are in the right. We make excuses for ourselves. We try to blame the other person. The last thing we normally do is actually admit that we have done something wrong. Little wonder that when we are faced with the challenge of the Eighth Step, we find it far easier to focus on the harm that has been done to us.

I often see this skewed focus when counseling couples who are planning to marry for the second time. One question I ask is, "How do you think you failed your partner in your previous marriage?" Almost inevitably they will tell me how *they* were hurt. They will explain how their partner had an affair or drank too much or didn't communicate or didn't meet their needs or always came home late. Seldom do they talk about the ways in which they hurt their ex-husband or ex-wife. Almost always they concentrate on the painful things that were done to them.

Now, I am the last person to stand in judgment on anyone else for doing this. In spite of trying to practice the Twelve Step program for several years now, I still catch myself focusing on the hurt done to me when my relationships get snarled up. In the words of a good friend, I get caught up in the PLOM syndrome (poor little old me).[1] Even in those moments when I am prepared to acknowledge outwardly that I have done something wrong, I still find myself thinking things like, "Well, I may have done this, but she did that," or "Yes, I may need to change, but he needs to change far more." Sound familiar?

The Eighth Step challenges us to deal with this deep-seated tendency in all of us to focus on how we have been hurt. While we most certainly are not responsible for all the pain that happens in our relationships (I think, for example, of someone who has been abused or raped), working out how we have harmed others is one of the most difficult challenges that we have to face if we want to relate in healthier and happier ways. One of the best methods of doing this, given our habits of denial and blaming, is to ask ourselves some tough questions. You will find some of these in the last part of this chapter.

BECOME WILLING TO
MAKE RESTITUTION

The second part of the Eighth Step asks us to become willing to make amends to the people we have harmed. This aspect scared me stiff when I first heard it. Perhaps it frightens you as well. However, before you decide to avoid this step, think about some of the possible benefits it might have for you. Here are just a few. Take a few moments to think about them. They may encourage you to be more open to take this step.

- Making restitution can help us to finally *get rid of those painful feelings that sometimes accompany our broken relationships*—feelings like guilt, remorse, shame, failure, resentment, anger, and even hatred. We begin to replace them with much more positive emotions when we set out on the road of making amends to those we have hurt.

- Making restitution can *release us from the grip of our past failures in loving others*. We become free to begin again. Because we have tried to put the record straight from our side, we can now focus our energies on becoming a more loving and less selfish person, able to concentrate on the present moment rather than always looking over our shoulder at yesterday's mistakes.

- Making restitution can *improve our health*. The medical profession has proved beyond doubt that unresolved emotional conflicts, resentments, fear, and guilt often cause physical ailments. When we work toward a greater harmony in our relationships, we increase the possibilities for health and wholeness.

- Making restitution can help us to *be more comfortable with the people from whom we have been estranged*. We will no longer always try to avoid them. We will be more relaxed in their presence. The air has been cleared between us. However they may ultimately respond, we know that we have done our best to clean up our side of the fence.

■ Making restitution can *open up our lives spiritually*. It can unblock the spiritual pipelines between God and ourselves. We will find ourselves caught up more powerfully in the flow of God's Spirit. Real changes will begin to take place, not only in the depths of our own lives, but also in the way we relate to and treat others.

When we think carefully about this list of possible benefits, one thing becomes clear. The act of making amends actually has more benefits for us than for the other person. If, in addition, the relationship is healed, it is an added bonus. But it is not the main reason we need to do so. We take Step Eight because it sets us free to love people more deeply and to do God's will more faithfully. As the Big Book of AA says about the practice: "Our real purpose is to fit ourselves to be of maximum service to God and the people about us."[2]

INTO ACTION

Step Eight says that we need to be willing to make amends to *all* those we have harmed. This sounds like an almost impossible challenge. As I write these words, I am deeply conscious that I have not made restitution to all the people on my amends list. Nonetheless, it is still my intention to try to do so. Somewhere in the Big Book of AA, it says that when we aim at the best, we always achieve something good in the end, even if we miss the bull's-eye. So let us begin the process of taking this step by asking God to help us reach out for the ideal. We can pray something like this:

Dear God, shine your light on all my relationships over the years. Show me where I have harmed others. I want to take responsibility for these hurts I have caused and be willing to make restitution. Where I am unwilling to do so, please help me to become more willing. Amen.

Our next step is actually to start drawing up our amends list. We need to be as specific, clear, and honest as we can. We must name the person whom we have hurt, describe our own harmful behavior, and try to be specific about the consequences we are aware of. So, for example, with regard to the story about my relationship with Debbie that I shared at the beginning of this chapter, I would like to note the following:

MY AMENDS LIST

Name of person	My harmful behavior	Consequences
Debbie	Took on too much work, failed to say no when necessary, and neglected to show my love and support.	Debbie felt left alone, unloved, and disconnected from me.

Making an amends list like this has powerful consequences. It will help us see ourselves more clearly. It will encourage us to stop making excuses. It will show us where we need to take remedial action. Most importantly, it will enable us to see how our character flaws affect others. Often these faults have been affecting our relationships negatively for years. Unless we deal with them proactively, they will continue to do so. Now that we have written them down on paper, we can start to ask God to help us overcome them.

As we write our amends list, we can also ask ourselves some hard questions—questions that will help us break through our tendency to blame and deny. Here are some that have helped me. You might like to add others to the list.

- When have I sought to dominate and control others?
- When have I been deceptive?
- When have I hurt others with my words?
- When have I withdrawn from others into a sulky silence?
- When have I not done what I said I would do?
- When have I been insensitive to the needs of others?

The aim of asking questions like these is not to go on a guilt trip. We simply want to get a clearer picture of how we have harmed others so that we can make amends.

Finally, what about those people who have hurt us? What are we going to do with them? Are we willing to step out on the road toward forgiving them? This is another challenge we need to face, otherwise we could spend the rest of our lives locked up in prisons of resentment, bitterness, and hatred. For this reason alone, before we move on to Step Nine we need to ask

God to help us also to forgive. It will mean learning to let go of our anger, to let go of our right to retaliate, and to let go of our quest for revenge. Extending forgiveness in this way may be one of the hardest things we ever do, but it is an absolutely essential part of the journey toward finding a more meaningful spirituality and becoming a whole human being.

TAKING IT FURTHER IN GROUP SHARING

1. Share one struggle you have in loving those close to you.
2. How do you feel about the concept of restitution?
3. Do you find it easy or difficult to acknowledge the hurts you have caused others?
4. What is your response to the invitation to take Step Eight?

STEP NINE

We made direct amends to such people wherever possible, except when to do so would injure them or others.

"So when you are offering your gift at the altar, if you remember that your brother or sister has something against you, leave your gift there before the altar and go; first be reconciled to your brother or sister, and then come and offer your gift."
—Matthew 5:23–24

RESTITUTION

H ere is a simple question. If someone steals something precious from you and then apologizes and asks you to forgive him or her, but does not return it or offer to replace it, how would you feel? Would you accept the apology? Would you think he or she is really sorry? I don't think so. Something important is missing. Something we call restitution, or making amends.

When it comes to putting right the things we have done wrong, we always need to try and make some form of restitution. Confession, forgiveness, and making amends all belong together, especially when we are also seeking to develop a better relationship with God. Any spiritual journey that overlooks the link among these three things runs the risk of being shallow and self-deceptive. Hence the absolute importance of Step Nine. Let me put it in my own words:

> *We must make restitution to all those we have harmed,*
> *provided that in doing so we do not bring further harm*
> *to them or to others.*

The Bible has some wonderful examples of people taking this step. Think for a moment of the well-known story in Luke 19:1–10 of

Zacchaeus, the little man who climbed up a tree in order to see Jesus. Do you remember what Zacchaeus did immediately after Jesus said he was coming to his house? He stood up and said, "If I have cheated anybody out of anything, I will pay back four times the amount" (Luke 19:8, NIV). His new spiritual experience went hand in hand with a deep desire to make restitution. He knew that there was no such thing as a private salvation deal with God. He had done wrong things to people that needed to be put right.

The Big Book of AA points out the huge benefits that come to those who are thorough at this stage of their Twelve Step journey. It says that when we make amends, we

> will not regret the past nor wish to shut the door on it. We will comprehend the word serenity, and we will know peace. . . . Our whole attitude and outlook upon life will change. Fear of people and of economic insecurity will leave us. We will intuitively know how to handle situations which used to baffle us. We will suddenly realize that God is doing for us what we could not do for ourselves.[1]

With these words to encourage us, let's go ahead and see what Step Nine involves.

MAKING DIRECT AMENDS
WHEREVER POSSIBLE

Restitution begins when we make a conscious decision to face those whom we have wronged. These people may include our spouses, parents, children, brothers and sisters, or close friends.

They may also include people we don't like, those with whom we don't communicate, even some whom we consider to be our enemies. We will be in regular contact with some of these people. Some we may not see at all. Step Nine invites us actually to go to them if it is possible, acknowledge the hurt we have caused them, and explain our desire to make amends.

I remember how I made amends to Debbie when she told me about the pain that I had caused through my constant absence from home. I sat down with her, apologized for neglecting our relationship, and explained my intention to put things right. I suggested that if she were willing, I would take her out every Monday night from then on. Depending on the budget, it would either be for a milk shake or a pizza. This practice continues today. Making restitution has been a lot of fun!

Sometimes it may not be enjoyable at all. A friend of mine with a gambling addiction had defrauded the company where he worked of large sums of money. When he began to take God seriously in his life, he knew that he needed to come clean. After long conversations with his family and trusted friends, he decided to own up. He went to his boss, admitted his wrongdoing, and offered to pay back with interest on a monthly basis what he had stolen. It has been a long, hard, and costly journey. Thankfully he was not fired or formally charged by his employers. Today my friend experiences a freedom and serenity that he had never known before.

It goes without saying that not all our attempts at making amends have happy endings. Some of those we approach may not be receptive. They may be too angry to see us or may tell us to get lost or may want to see us punished. Some may find it difficult to believe that we have genuinely turned over a new leaf.

Others may have been too deeply hurt by what we did to even consider any form of restitution. Whatever form the negative response may take, all we can do is accept that this is the way the person feels and try to move on. Our comfort will be in knowing that we did our very best to try to repair the damage of the past.

There will also be those situations where it is not possible to make direct amends. Maybe the person we wronged has died or lives somewhere else or cannot be traced. In cases like these we can only make "indirect amends." This means that by building our relationship with God; living the principles of the Twelve Steps as best we can; and seeking to become a less selfish, less controlling, and more loving human beings, we are putting matters right in an indirect way. We are saying to those we have hurt and to those to whom we have no immediate access, "I recognize that I have hurt you, but through my new way of life I am seeking to make it up to you indirectly."

WHEN NOT TO MAKE DIRECT AMENDS

Will you especially notice the second part of Step Nine? It says that we are to make direct amends to those whom we have harmed, "except when to do so would injure them or others" —in other words, we need to think very carefully before we take this step. What might the possible consequences of our making restitution be? If we could possibly cause greater harm, we must think twice before moving ahead. We must not expose someone else to more suffering just to ease our own conscience. We may have to live with our actions, accepting the fact that we can do nothing about them directly.

The Big Book of AA describes several possible examples where this may happen.[2] One concerns sexual infidelity. Let's say you had an affair. In order to straighten out your life with God and those around you, you embark on the Twelve Step journey. You have now arrived at Step Nine. What do you do? Do you tell your partner about the affair? Do you reveal the other person's name? What happens if this disclosure leads to further hurt for the other person? Before we just bring things out into the open, these dilemmas need to be considered carefully. In the end we may decide to make only a partial disclosure of what took place. At all times we must remember our guiding principle. Normally we are to make direct amends but never at another person's expense or when it will do more harm than we have already done.

Another example concerns a criminal offense. You have done something that, if disclosed, could land you in jail. What does Step Nine challenge you to do? Make full disclosure and take the consequences, even if that means devastation for your loved ones? The Big Book of AA offers a word of caution. It says that before taking any action that could seriously harm others, you first need to speak with them. Only after they have given permission should you disclose fully what you have done and carry the consequences.

What then can we do in the situations where we have decided not to make direct amends? We have some options. We can admit our wrongdoing in confidence to another person. We can accept God's forgiveness. We can remind ourselves that we wanted to make restitution but were unable to do so because it would cause further harm. We could resolve not to hurt anyone in the same way again. All these thoughts or actions will help us deal with the remorse and guilt that come from past wrongdoing. Finally, however, we have to learn to live with the consequences of what we have done, trusting that somehow God will use them to rebuild our lives and relationships.

The complexity of these two scenarios, and there are many others, underscore the tremendous value of having someone with whom we can talk things over: preferably someone who has already walked the restitution path—someone who can help us explore our dilemmas without trying to fix us up; someone who can be trusted to keep things in confidence; someone who will try to be objective about our situation. Sometimes this person could be the one to whom we made confession when we did Step Five. Without a person like this, it is highly improbable that we will manage to take this step.

INTO ACTION

Taking Step Nine involves at least three things. First of all, it requires the *right timing*. It's not advisable to run out and try to make restitution to everyone at once. We could end up hurting ourselves and others even more. Veteran Twelve Steppers suggest that we think carefully about the sequence in which we do things. They suggest that we start with the easiest situations, with those people whom we know are on our side. Usually these are loved ones who want the best for us. If we begin here, we can build some confidence and courage to tackle the more difficult and complex cases on our amends list. Otherwise we may not get started at all.

There is another reason why we need a healthy sense of timing. We may have harmed someone so badly that he or she is completely closed off to meeting with us. It's not advisable to approach someone who is hurting like this. Often it only makes matters worse. We need to bide our time and be patient. We can pray that God will help us discern when it would be best to reach out. I have found that God answers this prayer in surprising ways by providing us with the opportunity to connect with this person.

Second, it requires the *right approach*. When making amends, it does not help to come across in a religious or self-righteous way. Using lots of God language usually doesn't go down too well with people we have hurt. Nor do we want, in those situations where we have badly damaged a relationship by our words or actions, to give the impression that we are trying to go back to the relationship as it was. This is not the main reason we are taking this step. We want to make restitution because this is what we believe God asks of us.

How then do we approach the person whom we have hurt? We can go to him or her and say something like, "I know I have hurt you. I am really sorry for what I did. I want to do whatever I can to make amends. Can we talk about it?" If the other person wants to know why we are doing this, we might at that stage mention our spiritual journey. We could say, "I have given my life to God and am trying to get my life back on track. One of the things I know God wants me to do is to try to make up for what I did wrong."

Lastly, it will require the *right measures*. How do we ensure that we make amends in an appropriate way? Two questions can help us determine this. We can ask ourselves: "If I were in the other person's shoes, how would I want amends to be made?" Or we can put the question directly to the person whom we have hurt: "Is there any way in which I can make amends to you?" The response we get will give us some helpful clues about how we can give expression to our desire to make restitution.

Sometimes making amends will involve money. Maybe there is a loan we have not repaid. Or money we owe for goods. Or petty cash we took for our own use. In these cases we will have to approach those whom we have harmed financially and offer to repay whatever we can, even in installments. If there is a strong possibility that this could end up causing further pain to our loved ones, we must always talk things over with them first. Remember that this step asks us to make direct amends except when to do so will cause further injury.

Step Nine reminds us that when it comes to the hurt we have caused, we have a choice. We can run and hide, blame and deny, and try to pretend nothing is wrong. This response seldom contributes to our well-being or our growth. But there is another way to respond. We can face the facts, acknowledge what we have done and begin to make amends. When we choose to respond in this way, however imperfectly, we start to turn our lives toward the light of a new day dawning in our lives—a new day in which we begin to experience those gifts of peace and serenity and freedom for which our hearts long.

TAKING IT FURTHER IN GROUP SHARING

1. When have you made restitution in the past or been on the receiving end of someone else's act of restitution? How was this for you?
2. What do you think about the two examples where we need to be cautious about making direct amends? Can you think of any other examples where caution may be needed?
3. What is your response to the idea of making indirect amends?
4. What is your response to the invitation to take Step Nine?

STEP TEN

*We continued to take personal inventory
and when we were wrong
promptly admitted it.*

So if you think you are standing, watch out that
you do not fall.

—1 Corinthians 10:12

MAINTAINING PROGRESS

Once upon a time all the temptations were put on sale. Each one was packaged, priced, and advertised: the temptation to be selfish, to control those around us, to lose our temper, to nurse our grievances, to tell lies, to be greedy, and so on. Most of these were expensive. But there was one marked "Free." It was the temptation to be complacent. One day a customer came along, noticed this jar, and asked why it was being given away for nothing. "Oh, if you fall for that one," came the answer from behind the counter, "you are vulnerable to all the others."

Complacency is one of the most dangerous temptations on the spiritual journey, especially when we reach this stage of the Twelve Step program. Let me explain. If we have done the first nine steps, we should now be experiencing some wonderful benefits and blessings. These could range from experiencing a new awareness of God, a greater peace with ourselves, a lightness of heart to a much happier and more comfortable way of relating to those around us. Now comes the danger. It's the temptation to rest on our laurels and slip back into our usual life. We assume that we are fine, our life is back on track, and we don't need to do the steps any more.

Step Ten protects us from falling prey to this temptation. It does this in several ways. It reminds us to be aware of those character defects that we want to see changed. It alerts us to tensions and troubles in our relationships that may need our attention. It reinforces the fact that we will never stop needing God's help and power. Perhaps most importantly, it enables us to maintain progress in our spiritual journey, one day at a time. Here is what I think this step involves:

We must constantly reflect on our lives, acknowledging our mistakes, and attempting to put right immediately any wrong we may do.

This is not an invitation to continuous navel-gazing! Nor do we need to subject ourselves to neurotic self-surveillance. Rather, this is about doing all we can to keep ourselves growing personally and spiritually. The bottom line is that we must want to become the kind of person God can use to make this world a better and more caring place. This is the vision we can hold for our lives. But this kind of inner change does not happen overnight. It takes place gradually as we grow in self-awareness and in our capacity to say we are sorry quickly when we have harmed another person or done wrong. This is what the two parts of Step Ten are about. Let's look at each of them more closely.

CONTINUED TO MAKE
A PERSONAL INVENTORY

One simple sentence, spoken by Paul Welsh, my first supervisor in ministry over thirty years ago, still has a tremendous influence on the way I live today. His words have helped me understand how we get to know ourselves, deepen our spirituality, and become more loving and caring human beings. Each week during my first year of pastoral work, we sat in his study reviewing my daily activities. "Always remember," he said during one of these times, "we do not learn from experience, we learn when we *reflect* on our experience."

Those who drew up the Twelve Steps also knew this.[1] They were deeply aware that, unless we develop the habit of regular reflection, little personal or spiritual growth takes place in our life. We will keep making the same mistakes, repeating the same destructive behavior patterns, showing the same character defects. It is only when we take the time to reflect on how we are living that we open ourselves to the possibility of real character change. And so, as the first part of the Tenth Step puts it, we must regularly make a personal inventory. Here are a few methods that have proved to be helpful:

- We can do *regular spot checks*. We can do these throughout the day when we find ourselves in situations that disturb us or throw us off balance or tempt us to blow up in anger. In these moments we can learn to take a step back, think carefully about what is going on, and try to see how we may be contributing to the disturbance. The other person may be in the wrong too; but we can't change them, we can only make sure that our own reactions are positive ones.

■ We can do *regular nightly reviews*. At the end of each day, when we have a few available moments, we can look back on the past twenty-four hours and ask ourselves questions like: "Did I hurt anyone today?" "What did I do that hurt this person?" "Why did I do it?" "Which character defect of mine was in operation?" We can also look back on the main events of the day, taking note where we did things well and thanking God for the good things that happened to us.

■ We can do *long-term periodic inventories*. These happen best when we are away from our normal surroundings. We may be attending a conference, taking a short holiday, spending time at a favorite spot, or on a retreat. Often these times give us the breathing space we need to reflect more deeply on how our lives are going. We can see destructive patterns more clearly, spot problem areas, observe where we have made progress, and make new commitments for future growth. How often have you come back from a break determined to do things a bit differently?

I assure you that developing the habit of taking this continued inventory need not be a drag. In fact, it can become quite exciting. The more we reflect, the more we discover about ourselves. The more we discover about ourselves, the more we are able to offer to God. The more we offer to God, the more we can change for the better. We will begin to see that inner transformation really is possible. We do not have to stay the same for the rest of our lives. Nor do we need to suffer constant personal and spiritual defeat. We can make progress toward becoming the person God wants us to be.

WHEN WRONG, PROMPTLY ADMIT IT

The Tenth Step makes it clear that reflection by itself is not enough. If we want to keep making progress personally and spiritually, we need to build something else into our lives. We need to face up promptly to any wrong that we may do. We must admit it to ourselves and, if the need is there, also to the other parties concerned. This is an absolutely crucial part of the Tenth Step. Let me illustrate.

Some time ago I borrowed something from an acquaintance. When I had finished using it, I put it away, intending to return it. But I didn't. A few months later I received an e-mail from this person. He was angry that I had not returned the item as I had said I would. He said that "there is a name for people who borrow things without returning them." He was particularly upset because I had not given it to a couple from our congregation who had visited his area and who could have returned it on my behalf.

My immediate response was to try to justify myself. The best strategy, I thought to myself, would be to criticize him for his reaction. I wanted to defend my honorable intentions about returning the item and say that his accusation had been uncalled for. I also wanted to tell him that he had got his facts wrong. I did not know beforehand about the couple's visit to his area. My AA friends would have called what was going on in my mind "stinking thinking." Very deviously, I was trying to shift the focus from what I had not done to what he had done. To put it bluntly, I did not want to take responsibility for what I had failed to do.

In the midst of all these conflicting thoughts, I remembered the wisdom of the Tenth Step. I did a quick spot check. I reflected on what had taken place and asked myself if I had erred in any way. Of course I had. I had not returned the item as I had said I would. There was indeed a name for people who behaved like that. However, it was not enough for me merely to reflect on what I had done wrong. I also needed to admit it promptly to myself and to the other person. So I e-mailed him, acknowledged my slowness in getting the thing back, and promised to return it as soon as I could. Once I had done this, I felt at peace. I was able to put the matter to rest in my heart and get on with my life.

There was another consequence as well. After what had happened, I decided to do a wider check. I wanted to see if there were any other borrowed items that I had not yet returned. There were quite a few. An unpleasant fact began to stare me in the face. When it came to returning borrowed items, I was guilty of procrastination. Over recent months I have been trying to do something about this. I have been asking God to remove this character defect and to help me replace it with a greater promptness. I am happy to say that I have made some progress in this area.

I hope the Tenth Step is becoming a bit clearer to you. It does not mean going around continually saying sorry for every little thing. Nor is it about groveling in our guilt, beating ourselves over the head, or saying that we are useless. Rather, it involves looking honestly at our lives in the here and now, accepting responsibility for the wrong we have done or the good we have failed to do, and making full admission of these facts as quickly as we can. When we realize that we have done wrong, the sooner we can acknowledge it in this way, the better. We begin to carry less emotional baggage around with us and find that we are able to get on with living our lives.

INTO ACTION

Step Ten is sometimes referred to as the "maintenance step" of the Twelve Step Program. While the first nine steps help us to build new spiritual foundations, get to know ourselves better, confess our past wrongdoing, and show us where we need to make restitution, this step helps us maintain progress in our spiritual journey in the here and now. So let's begin right now to build the habit of constant reflection and immediate acknowledgment of wrongdoing into our daily lives. You can choose one of the following possibilities and do it right where you are.

- *Do a spot check.* Here is one suggestion. Using each of the letters from the word HEART, you can ask yourself:
  H = Am I Hurting?
  E = Am I Exhausted?
  A = Am I Angry?
  R = Am I Resentful?
  T = Am I Tense?
- If your answer to any of these questions is yes, quickly go through the first three steps again. Remember them. Admit your lack of power. Look beyond yourself to your Higher Power. Surrender yourself to God as you understand God to be. I have learned that doing this often brings me a clearer perspective of what I am going through, renews my connection with God, and guides my actions.
- *Do a nightly review.* Using the same list of character defects listed at the end of Step Six, check those that have surfaced over the past twenty-four hours. If any have, remember where it took place, and ask yourself whether you need to make an apology and/or amends. Here is the list:

Laziness	False pride	Defensiveness
Procrastination	Overspending	Lust
Overpromising	Prejudice	Impatience
Resentment	Hypercriticalness	Gluttony
Rationalization	Perfectionism	Touchiness
Manipulation	Worry	Unreliability
Phoniness	Greed	Self-pity
Irresponsibility	Ungratefulness	Self-centeredness
Gossip	Self-righteousness	Smugness
Dishonesty	Anger	Indifference
Blaming others	Racism	Apathy
Envy	Control	Suspicion

Once you have done this, do not forget to make a list of all the good things that have happened. Be as specific as you can. For example, as I sit here writing this chapter and looking back over the day I can think of many good things: a good sleep last night, an enjoyable cup of coffee early this morning, a special conversation with one of my children, a phone call from a friend, an instant message from Debbie who is away from home, a few moments of solitude watering the garden and enjoying the beauty of the spring colors.

■ *Do a longer-term periodic inventory.* You may need to save this exercise for the next time you are alone for a few hours. General questions like the following may help you evaluate your personal growth over the past few months.

- How has your relationship with God developed since the initial surrender of your life?
- How, since beginning the program, have you grown in self-awareness and self-knowledge?
- What burdens do you need to share or confess? Which of your character flaws seem to sneak up on you most often?
- What secret resentments do you keep hanging on to?

When we lose our ability to change, we can easily be physically alive but spiritually dead. This could be why God wants us to keep moving forward and deeper in our spiritual life. We are either growing or we are dying. The great gift of the Tenth Step is that it keeps us open to the channels of growing and changing. When we make it part of our daily routine, we can be sure that our life will never be dull but often fascinating, challenging, exciting, and awake to new possibilities. The secret, however, is maintaining progress, one day at a time.

TAKING IT FURTHER IN GROUP SHARING

1. Share one area of life where you are tempted to be complacent.
2. As a group, reflect in silence on the past twenty-four hours, using the questions suggested for the nightly review.
3. Share your experience of doing this silent reflection.
4. Do you find it easy or difficult to face up promptly to any wrong that you may have done?
5. What is your response to the invitation to take Step Ten?

STEP ELEVEN

*We sought through prayer and meditation
to improve our conscious contact with God . . . ,
praying only for knowledge of God's will
for us and the power to carry that out.*

> Going a little farther, [Jesus] threw himself on
> the ground and prayed, "My Father, if it is pos-
> sible, let this cup pass from me; yet not what I
> want but what you want."
>
> —Matthew 26:39

FINDING GOD'S WILL

A little boy was watching his granny rub some cream onto her face. He was intrigued and asked why she was doing this. She replied simply that she hoped the cream would take away her wrinkles. He became quiet, and continued to look closely at her face, obviously concerned. After a long silence, he said, "Granny, I'm sorry, but it's not working."

It is easy to have this attitude toward prayer, especially when we ask God to do something and nothing seems to happen. It may be a request to find a partner, to become pregnant, for a business deal to go through, for the health of a loved one to improve, or something else that we desperately want to see happen. Often in the painful shadow of unanswered prayers like these, we begin to wonder whether prayer really works. We find ourselves asking questions like, "Why do I bother to pray?" and "What am I supposed to pray for?" Sometimes we may even give up praying.

I often wrestle with these questions myself. In my search to find sensible answers I have read many books, listened to many talks, spoken to many people. All these have helped in some way, some more than others. What has helped most, however, has been the simple wisdom of the Eleventh Step. Here is how I would word it:

We must try to improve our connection with God through two-way communication, always asking that we may come to know and have the strength to do God's will.

This step describes clearly why we should pray and what we should pray for. Prayer works, as the Big Book of AA states, if we develop the proper attitude towards it.[1] I hope the following suggestions will encourage you to step out into a more meaningful journey of prayer, even if you have been disappointed by unanswered prayers in the past.

IMPROVE OUR CONSCIOUS CONTACT WITH GOD

Prayer works when we know *why* we pray. The first part of the Eleventh Step gives us a clear purpose for prayer. It suggests that the main reason we pray is to improve our conscious contact with God. The wording is careful and assumes that if we have been doing the other ten steps we will by now have some awareness of God working in our life. At this point, the program in effect says to us: "The time has come for you to deepen your connection with God, to make it stronger and more vital. The best way to do this is through prayer and meditation."

How do prayer and meditation connect us more deeply with God? To answer, let me offer a simple picture. Think of someone close to you. It could be your spouse, your child, your parent, or a good friend. If you want to strengthen your relationship with others, there needs to be open and honest two-way communication. Not only do you need to share yourself with the other persons, they also need to be able to share themselves with you. This dialogue is necessary for the growth of any human relationship. If communication is only one way, the relationship will definitely not grow.

In the same way, if we want to strengthen our connection with God, there needs to be two-way communication. On the one hand, we need to share ourselves openly with God. We call this talking to God *prayer*. Some may argue that it is a waste of time to tell God anything. After all, surely God knows everything about us already. However, it's not a question of giving new information to God. It's much rather a matter of trust and transparency—learning to speak openly with God about everything in our life and then experiencing the closeness that this kind of transparency brings to our relationship with God.

I remember learning how to do this. A close friend suggested that when I prayed I should put an empty chair near my bed. He told me to imagine Jesus sitting there and to speak with him as I would with a very good friend. I used this method regularly for a number of years. Sitting on the side of my bed, I would share with the Lord my deepest longings, my joys, my sorrows, my achievements, my shame. Sharing myself with Christ like this often brought me a deep sense of God's presence. While I don't use an empty chair any longer, to this day I continue speaking aloud with God whenever I pray. I imagine the Lord is present with me, and I seek to share honestly my thoughts and feelings, whatever they may be.

On the other hand, we also need to listen to God. If we understand *prayer* to be talking to God, then *meditation* can be described as listening to God. When we meditate, it simply means thinking about life and about things in God's presence. It could involve thinking about a passage from the Bible, our plans for the day that lies ahead, a problem or a conversation, or a character defect that keeps tripping us up. Whatever it is that we may decide to focus our thoughts on, the important thing in meditation is trying to hear what God may be saying so that we will end up doing what God wants us to do.

Almost every time I try to explain what meditation involves, someone will ask, "But how can I be sure that it is God speaking to me?" The answer is very simple. Thoughts influenced by God usually have a certain "feel" about them. They prompt us to do loving things, lead us in the direction of a more creative life, and invite us to take better care of ourselves. They never accuse or condemn but often urge us toward a better way of doing things. They draw us into a closer walk with God. Learning to discern the divine whisper in our thoughts can become one of our greatest adventures in life.

PRAYING ONLY FOR KNOWLEDGE OF GOD'S WILL FOR US AND FOR THE POWER TO CARRY IT OUT

Prayer works when we know *what* to pray for. The second part of this step gives us a clear focus. It suggests that we focus on a knowledge of God's will and the power to carry it out. This is the Twelve Step program's main insight on prayer. We do not pray just to get God to do what we want. We pray so that we get to know God's will and find the strength to do it. Jesus exemplifies this when he prays to his Father in the garden of Gethsemane: "'Not as I will, but as you will'" (Matt. 26:39, NIV).

Now, in one respect there is no great mystery surrounding the will of God. Generally speaking, we know what God wants. We know that God wants us to be loving, to be honest, to serve others, to use our gifts, and to do as much good as we can. What we still need to know, however, is what God's general will may mean to us in specific situations in our everyday lives. When we pray for this knowledge, it often happens that God gives us special insights and promptings that enrich our lives and the lives of those around us. We begin to live and act in a way that is in line with God's will and purpose for us.

This focus of praying to know God's will has made a huge difference in the way I pray. For years I assumed that I knew what was best for myself and others. I would then ask God to bring about what I wanted to see done. When this didn't happen, I would think that my prayers were not working. Today I pray in a very different way. Rather than tell God what to do in a specific situation, I ask God how I need to respond. "Lord, please show me your will and give me the strength to do it," has become an almost daily prayer for me.

Praying like this does not always mean that we will get an answer in bright neon lights or on a computer printout; nor does it mean that everything will work out smoothly, neatly, and tidily. God's will usually shows itself to us gradually. My experience is that we may receive just enough light to know what to do next. Like a handheld lamp that lights up the next few steps along a dark pathway, God gives us just enough light to keep walking. As we walk in the light we are given, another bit of illumination will come along, guiding us further. And so we proceed, one step at a time, one day at a time. All the time we keep trusting that God is lovingly walking with us in whatever it is we are going through.

"But suppose no clear guidance comes," you may ask, "what then?" When this happens, we need to assume that it may be

God's will for us to take responsibility and make up our own minds. God has given us the good gifts of common sense, reason, and the ability to think. Using all these gifts, we then try to decide how we can best be faithful to God's general will. In moments like these, when no clear light is shed on our specific situations, our choices and decisions reveal whether our lives have really been surrendered to God or not.

INTO ACTION

When it comes to putting the Eleventh Step into practice, it's hard to improve on what the Big Book of AA suggests.[2] These suggestions are described so well that I suspect the writers were guided by God in what they wrote. The down-to-earth language outlines clearly what a daily discipline of prayer and meditation can look like. Here are their suggestions with some of my thoughts as well:

- In the evening, the writers suggest a *nightly review*. In the previous chapter I gave one way of doing this. You might like to read it again. The important thing about praying at night is to reflect on God's presence on the day gone by. We should give thanks for everything that was good, apologize for where we went wrong, and ask God to show us where we need to put things right. Simple prayer like this keeps our connection with God alive. It also helps us to sleep better and to wake up feeling closer to God.
- In the morning the writers suggest that we *think about the day facing us*. We could ask God to direct our lives. If we are facing specific situations that make us worried or afraid, we could consciously place them in God's hands for the next

twenty-four hours and ask for the help and guidance we need. Here is one way you could build this morning prayer time. It is the "five P" approach to prayer.

- *Place*: Find a place where you can be uninterrupted and have quality time alone with God. Close human relationships are always nurtured by special places. So too with God. Therefore ask yourself: *Where is the best place for me to pray, given the actual circumstances of my life?*
- *Prepare*: Take some time to settle down before you begin your time of meditation and prayer. You might like to breathe deeply for a few moments. Breathe in the presence of God and breathe out whatever negative feelings you may have. Have a lighted candle to look at sometimes or listen to some soothing music or quietly repeat a chosen word that describes God for you.
- *Passage*: Read slowly a portion from one of your favorite devotional books. The book through which God most often speaks to me is the Bible. Often when I read or reread a scripture passage, a word or phrase or sentence stands out for me and invites my attention.
- *Ponder*: Spend a few minutes in silence, thinking more deeply about what you have read. Ask what it might mean for your life, especially in the light of the day that lies ahead. Imagine what your life might look like if you were to put this new insight into immediate practice.
- *Prayer*: Talk to God about whatever you are thinking and feeling. Thank God for specific persons or things. Ask God to help you understand what you are to do during the next twenty-four hours and to give you the power to

carry it out. Commit yourself to God again, along with all the things that you are anxious and concerned about in the day ahead.

■ During the day the writers suggest that we *direct our thoughts as often as we can toward God*. When familiar character defects appear, we could ask God to remove them. When we are confronted with situations where we really do not know what to do or when we feel frantic and uptight, we could renew our focus by saying quietly, "Your will, not mine be done." When things go well, or some good comes our way, we could thank God. To quote the well-known words of Brother Lawrence, we must try to "practice the presence of God" in all these different ways.

However much we have emphasized the value of prayer and meditation in this chapter, we should never neglect the importance of action. It is not enough merely to ask God for a knowledge of the divine will—we must act on whatever light we receive. We may pray, but it is still our responsibility to do the legwork. Only then will the power of God flow through us. As one AA writer put it: "We ask for God's Will for us through verbal prayer; we learn God's Will for us through meditation; we do the Will of God by action."[3] When these three things come together, prayer really works!

TAKING IT FURTHER IN GROUP SHARING

1. How would you describe your God-connection at the moment?
2. Share one struggle that you experience in prayer and meditation.
3. What did you find most helpful in this chapter for your own practice of prayer and meditation?
4. What is your response to the invitation to take Step Eleven?

STEP TWELVE

*Having had a spiritual awakening
as a result of these steps, we tried to carry
this message to [others] and to practice
these principles in all our affairs.*

[Jesus] said to him, "Go home to your friends,
and tell them how much the Lord has done for
you, and what mercy he has shown you."
—Mark 5:19

SHARING THE MESSAGE

Before we explore the Twelfth Step, here is a question for you. Please take a few moments to think about your answer. In what specific way(s) have you changed so far as a result of doing the Twelve Step program?

I ask this question for a simple reason. The Twelfth Step, as we shall see, consists of three parts. Two of them make definite suggestions about what we need to do if we want to keep progressing spiritually. In contrast, the first part describes what has most likely happened for those of us who have tried to put into practice the first eleven steps. It confidently asserts that we will have had some kind of spiritual awakening. What an incredible promise for anyone who takes the Twelve Step journey seriously. I wonder if this has happened for you.

HAVING HAD A
SPIRITUAL AWAKENING

What does it mean to have a "spiritual awakening"? It sounds awfully "religious." To put it simply, a spiritual awakening means coming alive in some area of our life where previously there was a deadness. It is a deeply personal thing. No two people awaken spiritually in the same way. God's Spirit always works uniquely in each one of us. Here are a few different ways in which we may have been renewed.

- We may have become more *accepting of who we really are.* We may have become more aware of our gifts and talents and what we can offer to others, or we may have a deeper awareness of our own self-centeredness and our compulsive need to control others.
- We may have come to *enjoy our more positive emotions.* We may feel a new joy in living, a deeper peace at the core of our being, a greater sense of gratitude for all the good things in our life, or a fresh hope for the future.
- We may have found a *new freedom in our capacity for choice.* We don't feel like hopeless victims any longer, trapped in the mistakes of the past. Instead, we have become more determined to think and choose and to do things that we weren't able to do before.
- We may have experienced *new life in our relationships.* We are less caught up in our own little world and are more willing to extend ourselves to others. We find that we are able to relate more openly and freely with those around us.
- We may have come to *appreciate the gift of life*—to hear the sound of wind in the trees, to smell the scent of a beautiful rose, to enjoy the taste of a good meal, to delight in the playfulness of a puppy. Our senses are awake again.
- We may have become more *aware of the divine presence in and around us.* We feel that we are in touch with a source of power and strength from beyond ourselves. We know now

that we have a loving, caring, and merciful God who walks with us, whatever we may be going through: Someone who never leaves or forsakes us.

Can you identify with any of these? If you can, then you have had a spiritual awakening. The Twelfth Step now suggests that we need to do two further things if we want to continue growing into the person God wants us to be. Here is how I would express it:

> *We need to pass on the good news we have experienced and implement the spiritual values of the Twelve Steps in the whole of our lives.*

WE TRIED TO CARRY THIS MESSAGE TO OTHERS

I still remember the first bit of spiritual advice I ever received. I had just made my first public commitment to Jesus Christ and was sitting with one of the counselors after the service. We were discussing how I could nourish my faith and grow in my new relationship with God. After showing me some biblical passages that underlined the importance of making a conscious surrender of my life to God, and explaining the need for regular habits of Bible reading and prayer, my counselor extended a parting challenge.

"Make sure that you tell someone soon about the step you have taken tonight."

"But why must I do that?"

"If you don't share with others what you have received, you will lose what you have been given."

My counselor knew something that we often overlook. When we have experienced spiritual renewal and healing, we need to pass on to someone else what we have received because when we do this our faith continues to grow and deepen. And when we don't, it often shrivels up and dies. The authors of the Twelve Step program were also aware of this. They knew that to keep the strength, sanity, and serenity received through doing the steps, we need to share our experience. Hence their wording of the Twelfth Step: "Having had a spiritual awakening as a result of these steps, we tried to carry this message to [others]."

How do we go about doing this in practical ways? Certainly not by trying to force others to believe in exactly the same way as we do nor by attempting to "fix" the people around us with our solutions and prescriptions for their lives. The Twelfth Step does not tell us to try to change anyone else. It simply asks us to try to carry the message to others, sharing our experience with those around us and passing on the good news. We tell our story with gentleness, honesty, and courtesy. Someone once said that passing on the good news is like "one beggar telling another beggar where he or she can find some bread."[1]

Opportunities to share our personal experiences of God and of following the program usually come only after we have tried to get to know people on their own terms. This means taking a genuine interest in them and in what they are saying and experiencing, instead of looking for gaps in the conversation to speak about our own spiritual journey. I am aware that this may sound contradictory to the ideas that some of us who are Christians have about "spreading the Word." However, I have learned over the years that the best way of sharing the message is to keep quiet and listen before we speak. When we listen before we speak, we get a much better hearing when we do say something.

Of course, this is not the only way we can communicate the message to others. There are many other possibilities: We can tell our story during a church service, or at our Twelve Step group, if we belong to one; we can invite someone who is struggling with an addiction to a group like AA, Narcotics Anonymous, or Overeaters Anonymous. Or we can befriend a newcomer to the program and share our experience of the different steps. By writing this book, and exploring with you the relevance of the Twelve Steps for nonalcoholics, I am doing exactly this: trying to pass on the good news that I have personally experienced.

AND TO PRACTICE THESE
PRINCIPLES IN ALL OUR AFFAIRS

There is one more thing the Twelfth Step asks us to do. Having had a spiritual awakening through surrendering ourselves to God and doing the steps, we need to widen the lens and try to "practice these principles in all our affairs." In other words, we are challenged to take the different spiritual values of the program and implement them in the whole of our lives. We can begin to use them in our financial affairs, in our relationships, in our business dealings, in our sexual conduct, and so on. As we seek to do this, the miracle of transformation spreads through every part of our lives.

In his book *A Hunger for Healing,* Keith Miller gives us a helpful picture of how to do this.[2] Try to think of the principles of the Twelve Steps as a bag of spiritual golf clubs, he suggests. As any golfer knows, when you want to choose a club, you first look at the situation you are in and then decide which club to use. In the same way, when we try to practice the principles, we look at the situation we are in and then we pull out the spiritual golf club that we most need. The principle that we choose to put into practice depends on where we are, what we are facing, and where we are hoping to go.

Here is an example. In a few weeks' time my youngest child will be leaving to work overseas as an exchange student. As the time of his departure draws nearer, I have mixed emotions. On one hand, I'm happy for him. Here is an opportunity to leave behind his childhood safety nets and begin to explore life on his own. On the other hand, it will not be easy for me to let go. While I know in my head that it's important for him to do this, a part of me wants him to stay behind where I can keep a protective eye on him!

As a Twelve Stepper I need to implement the spiritual values of the Twelve Step program within this particular situation. So, to go back to Keith Miller's golfing analogy, I select the spiritual golf club that best fits the issue I am facing.

The one that seems most relevant is the principle linked with Step Three. It's the principle of surrendering our will and our life, of not "playing God," of letting go and letting God be God. Practicing the principles of the Twelve Steps in all my affairs means that in this instance I take my hands off my son and keep placing him in God's hands. By doing this, I give him the space to become the kind of person that he wants to be.

The Twelve Step program contains wise principles that show us how we can live well. If we put them into practice in all our affairs, we will experience tremendous benefits and blessings. We will experience a growing sense of sanity and serenity that we will not have known before. We will begin to have small victories over those weaknesses that were once sabotaging our lives and relationships. We will move beyond being superficial in our relationship with God. In the words of the final line of one of the short stories in the Big Book of AA: "At last, I was at peace with myself. And with others. And with God."[3]

INTO ACTION

With the last step, as with all the others, action is the magic word. It's always by stepping out in faith and actually doing what the program suggests that we come to understand it. Two easy exercises will help us put the Twelfth Step into action.

The first is to sit down and write an up-to-date story of how God has used the Twelve Step program to bring about change in your life. Your story will have three parts. Begin by making a note of a real-life weakness you were struggling with before you started doing the steps. It may have been a struggle with some form of addiction, compulsive behavior, a tendency to control those around you, or a losing battle with worry or fear or some other negative emotion.

Then, write down what prompted you to start doing the Twelve Steps. How did the idea come to you? What was it like for you to set out on this journey?

Once you have done this, put down on paper how your life has changed. It does not have to be a total success story, but in what way is your life a little better than it was?

When you have finished this exercise, you have in your hands your own personal story, ready to share with anyone who may need to hear it.

The second exercise concerns selecting the principle or step you most need to practice in your life at this moment. Remember the analogy of the spiritual golf bag? Each step embodies certain values that you can implement. Which one do you most need to use right now? For convenience, here is a combined list of the different principles associated with the Twelve Steps:

Step One: Admitting weakness, acknowledging powerlessness
Step Two: Looking to a Higher Power beyond ourselves, believing that God really cares
Step Three: Surrendering our will and our lives, giving up "playing God," letting go and letting God
Step Four: Facing ourselves, examining our lives honestly, growing in self-awareness
Step Five: Coming clean, sharing honestly with others, asking for feedback
Step Six: Willingness to change
Step Seven: Learning to ask, acquiring humility
Step Eight: Accepting that we have hurt others, becoming willing to make restitution
Step Nine: Making restitution, taking responsibility for what we have done
Step Ten: Daily reflection, ongoing self-examination and self-awareness
Step Eleven: Prayer and meditation, seeking God's will
Step Twelve: Serving others, sharing what we have experienced, passing on the Twelve Step message

You have already practiced these principles in your life and experienced their power to change your life. Now, think about the actual circumstances of your own life at the moment and choose one principle that could be helpful in your daily life.

In closing, may I share with you one last time what I believe is God's vision for your life. It comes from Galatians 5:22-23. God would love you to become a more loving, joyful, peaceful, patient, kind, good, faithful, gentle, and self-controlled person. If you really want to reach out to this breathtaking vision, you have been given a wonderful gift to help you access the power that makes this possible. It is the gift of the Twelve Steps. They often say at AA, "It's a God-given program." I have discovered this to be more than true. As you seek to do the steps, with God's help, I hope you will discover it too.

TAKING IT FURTHER IN GROUP SHARING

1. Share one way in which you feel you have come alive since you have put the Twelve Steps into practice.
2. Have you ever been put off by someone talking about their faith? What can you learn from this?
3. What principle of the Twelve Step program do you most need to practice at the moment?
4. What is your response to the invitation to take Step Twelve?

BIBLIOGRAPHY

Al-Anon's Twelve Steps and Twelve Traditions. Virginia Beach, Va.: Al-Anon Family Group Headquarters, 1981.

Alcoholics Anonymous: The Story of How Many Thousands of Men and Women Have Recovered from Alcoholism, 3rd ed. New York: Alcoholics Anonymous World Services, 1976.

de Mello, Anthony. *Taking Flight: A Book of Story Meditations.* New York: Doubleday, 1988.

Doe, Father John [Ralph Pfau]. *Sobriety and Beyond.* Center City, Minn.: Hazelden Publishing and Educational Services, 1955.

_____. *Sobriety without End.* Center City, Minn.: Hazelden Publishing and Educational Services, 1997.

Father Fred and the Twelve Steps: A Primer for Recovery. Worcester, Mass.: Ambassador Books, 1996.

Joe McQ. *The Steps We Took: A Teacher of the Twelve Steps Shares His Experience, Strength, and Hope with All Those Recovering from Addictions, All Who Want to Recover, and All Who Love Them.* Blue Ridge Summit, Pa.: August Publishers, 2002.

Miller, J. Keith. *Hope in the Fast Lane.* (New York: HarperCollins Publishers, 1991).

_____. *A Hunger for Healing: The Twelve Steps as a Classic Model for Christian Spiritual Growth.* New York: HarperCollins Publishers, 1992.

Monahan, Molly. *Seeds of Grace: A Nun's Reflections on the Spirituality of Alcoholics Anonymous.* Farmington Hills, Mich.: Thomson Gale, 2001.

Willard, Dallas. *Renovation of the Heart: Putting on the Character of Christ.* Colorado Springs, Col.: NavPress, 2002.

NOTES

INTRODUCTION: MAPPING OUR JOURNEY
1. Dallas Willard, *Renovation of the Heart: Putting on the Character of Christ* (Colorado Springs, Colo.: NavPress, 2002), 85.

2. *Alcoholics Anonymous: The Story of How Many Thousands of Men and Women Have Recovered from Alcoholism,* 3rd ed. (New York: Alcoholics Anonymous World Services, 1976), 83.

3. Trevor Hudson, *The Serenity Prayer* (Cape Town, South Africa: Struik Christian Books, 2002).

STEP TWO: HOPE FOR CHANGE
1. *Alcoholics Anonymous,* 47.

STEP THREE: DECISION TIME
1. *Alcoholics Anonymous,* 60–61.

2. Dallas Willard develops this view about the will in *Renovation of the Heart,* 141–57.

3. J. Keith Miller, *The Secret Life of the Soul* (Nashville, Tenn.: Broadman and Holman Publishers, 1997), 3.

STEP FOUR: DARING TO FACE OURSELVES
1. *Alcoholics Anonymous,* 64–71.

STEP SIX: READY AND WILLING
1. See Romans 7:15-20; 1 Corinthians 2:3-5; 2 Corinthians 12:7-10.

2. I came across this analogy in the writings of Richard Foster.

STEP SEVEN: THE QUEST FOR HUMILITY
1. J. Keith Miller, *A Hunger for Healing: The Twelve Steps as a Classic Model for Christian Spiritual Growth* (San Francisco: HarperSanFrancisco, 1992), 116.

2. For example, see Jesus' teachings in Luke 11:1–13.

3. Anthony de Mello, *Taking Flight: A Book of Story Meditations* (New York: Doubleday, 1988), 114–15.

4. Dallas Willard develops this concept of humility in some of his talks.

5. *Alcoholics Anonymous,* 76.

STEP EIGHT: REFLECTING ON OUR RELATIONSHIPS
1. I heard this expression mentioned by a practicing psychiatrist, Dr. Cliff Allwood.

2. *Alcoholics Anonymous,* 77.

STEP NINE: RESTITUTION
1. *Alcoholics Anonymous*, 83–84.
2. *Alcoholics Anonymous*, 78–82.

STEP TEN: MAINTAINING PROGRESS
1. See Al-Anon's *Twelve Steps and Twelve Traditions* (Virginia Beach, Va.: Al-Anon Family Group Headquarters, 1981), 63–68.

STEP ELEVEN: FINDING GOD'S WILL
1. *Alcoholics Anonymous*, 86.
2. *Alcoholics Anonymous*, 86–88.
3. Father John Doe [Ralph Pfau], *Sobriety and Beyond* (Indianapolis, Ind.: SMT Guild, 1955), 173.

STEP TWELVE: SHARING THE MESSAGE
1. This saying is often attributed to D. T. Niles.
2. Miller, *A Hunger for Healing,* 211.
3. *Alcoholics Anonymous*, 561.

The following constitutes an extension of the copyright page